Longman Practice Exam Papers

A-level
Business Studies

Barry Brindley
Martin Buckley

Series editors:

Geoff Black and Stuart Wall

Titles available for A-Level

Biology

Business Studies

Chemistry

Physics

Psychology

Pure Mathematics and Mechanics

Pure Mathematics and Statistics

Addison Wesley Longman Limited
Edinburgh Gate, Harlow
Essex CM20 2JE, England
and Associated Companies throughout the World

First published 1999

ISBN 0-582-36920-7

British Library Cataloguing in Publication Data
A catalogue record for this book is available from the British Library

Set in Times 11/13 and Gill Sans by 38

Printed in Singapore

Contents

How to use this book

There are two examination papers divided into three parts. Part 1 of each paper consists of structured questions based on mini case studies. This is a typical format of questions for many of the examination boards. Part 2 is a series of short-answer questions on each of the main core topics. Although you will not meet a paper devoted solely to such questions they often form part of structured questions or the start of case studies. It is important to know the definitions and examples accurately.

Part 3 is an extended case study. There are two varieties to match the types used by the different examination boards. Paper 1 uses a structured approach with one essay while Paper 2 demands an extended report and two essays.

You can use the papers in a variety of ways. Parts 1 and 3 form a typical two-paper examination format used by many of the boards. These could be attempted in full in the time indicated just like a mock examination. Alternatively you could adopt a topic approach by attempting all of the questions on a single topic; for example, marketing. The matrix below is designed to help you in this and traces topics through each paper. To do this successfully you will first have to pre-read the case studies. If you also want to restrict the time taken then allow approximately one and a half minutes per mark allocated to the question.

Whichever method you choose, make sure that you have sufficient time, a quiet working area and a specific goal for the task. Marking the papers with a friend who has done a similar task is a good way of talking through areas where you have underscored.

	Paper 1				*Paper 2*			
	Part 1	*Part 2*	*Part 3*		*Part 1*	*Part 2*	*Part 3*	
			Section A	*Section B*			*Section A*	*Section B*
Objectives and the business environment	Q1aii,iii,iv Q5b	Q1–5	Q1 Q3 (also M and A + F)	Q1 also HR Q2	Q1d Q2d Q4a,d	Q1–5	Applies to all parts of the syllabus	Q2a,b Q6 (also HR)
Marketing	Q2c Q4c Q6a,bii	Q1–6	Q3		Q3c Q5a–c Q5d	Q1–6	Applies to all parts of the syllabus	Q1
Accounting and finance	Q1ai Q4a,b Q5a Q6bii	Q1–7	Q2a,b Q6a,b Q3		Q1a–c Q3a,b Q6d	Q1–5	Applies to all parts of the syllabus	Q3a,b
Human resources	Q1biii	Q1–5	Q4 Q5	Q1	Q4b,c Q6c	Q1–5	Applies to all parts of the syllabus	Q5a,b Q6
Operations management	Q1bi,ii Q2a,b Q3a–d Q6b	Q1–5			Q2a–c Q6a,b	Q1–5	Applies to all parts of the syllabus	Q4a–c

Remember to set yourself a goal, put effort into achieving it and where improvement is noticed CONGRATULATE yourself!

Examination questions

Whatever board you are being examined by you will find that there are several different types of examination question you may be faced with. Here, our aim is to introduce you to the kinds of questions you may face and provide some helpful guidelines in tackling them.

Short-answer questions

These are also referrred to as 'restricted response' questions and most exam boards will include some of these.

Short-answer questions are designed to test your knowledge across the whole of the syllabus. It is an attempt to make sure that you have covered the syllabus rather than just concentrating on certain areas. The questions are designed to test recall and comprehension of material. Contrary to popular opinion, this is not an easy part of the examination *unless you have the necessary breadth of knowledge*.

In answering these questions an understanding of mark allocation is important. Where, for example, only 2 or 3 marks are given, little in the way of development is required. So, if you come across a question such as:

> *'State 2 barriers to a firm entering the export market'* **(2 marks)**

a short or terse reply, such as:

- *difficulties with language*
- *no knowledge of distribution channels*

is sufficient.

Command verbs such as *give, name, outline* and *list* require the same treatment – a short answer with little development.

Other short-answer questions with a greater mark allocation require you to go further than a statement without explanation. Command words such as *compare, define, describe, explain, how* and *why* indicate that a fuller treatment is required.

Data-response questions

These questions present you with a 'real-life' situation on which a number of questions can be asked. Many of these questions will be based on quantitative information requiring you to produce a solution. Common failings here include:

- lack of practice in manipulating quantitative information to produce a solution
- failure to show workings
- an inability to interpret the results of your calculations.

Another form of data-response question is where you are required to comment on a passage of writing. For example a question such as

> *'What arguments has the Marketing Manager put forward to justify a change in pricing policy?'*

requires you to identify and state the relevant facts of the passage.

Common failings here result from the introduction of extraneous information not included in the passage and the consequent loss of time and missing of relevant points.

Finally, data-response questions may invite you to consider information that is not included in the case study. An example is:

> *'What other factors should the owner consider before deciding whether to expand his business?'*

These questions are designed to test your wider knowledge of the syllabus ... but as importantly relate it to the situation in the data-response material. In fact it is the student's inability to apply knowledge to the context of the situation that is the most common failing.

Case-study questions

This is a simulation of a 'real-life' situation. Like most real-life situations, there is insufficient information, there is irrelevant information and there is commonly no clearly correct answer. The examiner expects your answers to be in the context of the case study but to show your understanding of business ideas, concepts and theories in substantiating your arguments.

Whether the case study is issued prior to the examination or on the day, the same process of analysis should be undertaken. This is often referred to as a SWOT analysis. S and W refer to the internal **S**trengths and **W**eaknesses of the organisation; O and T refer to the **O**pportunities and **T**hreats arising from the environment the organisation works in.

Strengths and Weaknesses should be considered in relation to each of the functional departments within the organisation – particularly marketing, finance, operations and human resources (though there may be others depending on the case study. Similarly, Opportunities and Threats may be analysed through a consideration of the social, legal, economic, political and technological environments facing the organisation.

You will often find that there are certain key factors within a case study. An understanding of these limited issues and the application of business concepts and theories to them is often sufficient to obtain high marks. This is illustrated by the 'levels of response' mark scheme, adopted by most examination boards and used extensively in this book for more 'valuable' questions.

Levels of response mark schemes indicate that to obtain higher marks you must demonstrate the more difficult skills such as analysis and evaluation. A typical 8-mark question would have a mark scheme as follows:

LEVEL 1	one or more relevant points without development	1–3 marks
LEVEL 2	analyses one or more points in the context of the question	4–6 marks
LEVEL 3	evaluates points made	7–8 marks.

To obtain the highest marks you will need to practise analysing problems, developing alternative solutions and recommending courses of action.

In practice this may sound almost impossible – there are so many imponderables. And you are quite right! What the examiner is looking for is the ability to take facts and apply theory or business concepts in order to substantiate your conclusion. You should realise that in the majority of case-study questions there is *no* right answer and the examiner will award high marks for a well-thought-out and well-presented argument even though he or she may personally disagree with it.

Essay questions

Examination boards seem to be moving away from the free-response or essay question, but the following comments are also useful when answering case-study questions.

- Define any terms you use.
- Answer the question set – not the one you expected!
- Many questions are deliberately vague. You should explain the approach you are taking.
- Where possible, support your answer with business concepts and theory.
- Support your answer by the use of well-known examples.
- Consider both sides of the argument. Where contentious issues are involved, many students consider only one side of the argument.
- Consider all aspects of the question. If the firm is the basis of the study use your SWOT analysis to make sure you don't miss points.

Editors' preface

Longman Practice Exam Papers are written by experienced GCSE examiners and teachers. They will provide you with an ideal opportunity to practise under exam-type conditions before your actual school or college mocks or before the GCSE examination itself. As well as becoming familiar with the vital skill of pacing yourself through a whole exam paper, you can check your answers against examiner solutions and mark schemes to assess the level you have reached.

Longman Practice Exam Papers can be used alongside *Longman GCSE Study Guides* and *Longman Exam Practice Kits* to provide a comprehensive range of home study support as you prepare to take your GCSE in each subject covered.

Acknowledgements

We would like to thank our wives and families for their enduring patience during the writing process of this our fourth joint venture. Without their help and encouragement this writing partnership could not exist. Thanks must also go to Caroline Lipman, Fran Heatley, Caroline Wilson and Jo Lee of Leeds Girls' High School who tested these papers as part of their revision programme. Their constructive comments have formed part of the final version.

Longman Examination Board

General Certificate of Education

Business Studies Advanced

Paper 1

Part 1

Time: 3 hours

Number	Mark
1.	
2.	
3.	
4.	
5.	
6.	
Total:	

Instructions

■ Paper 1, Part 1, has 6 questions. **Answer 4 questions only**.

■ Answer questions on separate ruled paper.

■ Show all stages in any calculation, and state the units.

■ Where diagrams are required, make sure they are drawn and labelled clearly.

Information for candidates

■ You are allowed 3 hours for Paper 1, Part 1.

■ The marks available are shown in brackets after each question or part-question.

■ The maximum mark for Paper 1, Part 1, is 100.

---

1. Softies Ltd is a UK importer of large soft toys that are manufactured at its factory in Taiwan. Its products are distributed through a wholesaler to a variety of retail outlets from department stores to small 'corner shops'.

   (a) The biggest selling item is the Giant Panda. The wholesale price is £9, labour and material costs together are £4 per unit, allocated fixed costs are £2,000,000 and the current output and sales are both 700,000 units.

      (i) Calculate the break-even level of output and the margin of safety. **(2 marks)**

      (ii) If the wholesale price fell by £2 Softies estimates that sales would rise to 950,000 units. Calculate and comment on the price elasticity of demand for the product.
      (3 marks)

      (iii) Outline the usefulness of price elasticity of demand **and** break-even analysis for Softies **in this context**.

      (6 marks)

      (iv) Explain how a fluctuating exchange rate might present problems to Softies.
      (4 marks)

   (b) Softies currently manufactures its toys using a batch production method but is investigating the use of flow production for popular items such as the Giant Panda.

      (i) Explain briefly the terms 'batch' and 'flow production'. **(2 marks)**

      Turn over

      1

    (ii) Outline the advantages for Softies in changing to a flow production system.

                                        (4 marks)

    (iii) Examine any **two** human resource management problems associated with the introduction of flow production, and how Softies might approach them.

                                        (4 marks)

2. Cool Sports Ltd order skateboards from a manufacturer over the 8-week period beginning 1.1.98. Stock on that day was 60 units and Cool Sports always re-order when stocks fall to 30 units. For the first $4\frac{1}{2}$ weeks, stocks were depleted at 20 units per week; for the next $2\frac{1}{2}$ weeks, at 40 units per week; and the last week, at 35 per week.

During the 8-week period deliveries were received as shown in the table below.

Order no.	Delivery size in units	Time lag between re-order and delivery
1	80	1 week
2	60	$\frac{1}{2}$ week
3	40	$\frac{1}{2}$ week

  (a)   (i) Using graph paper draw a diagram to show the stock usage of skateboards over the 8-week period.   **(7 marks)**

         (ii) What is the closing stock figure at the end of week 8?   **(1 mark)**

         (iii) State **two** assumptions underlying your graph which might be considered unrealistic.

                                          (2 marks)

  (b)   (i) Define the term 'buffer stock'. Outline **three** factors which Cool Sports Ltd would take into account when setting the buffer stock level.   **(4 marks)**

         (ii) Cool Sports Ltd set a buffer stock level of 20 skateboards and normally order in batches of 80. Give **two** reasons that might explain why the level of stock fell below this during week 7 and week 8.   **(2 marks)**

  (c)   (i) How might the concept of the Product Life Cycle assist a manufacturer of consumer durables in determining stock levels throughout the life of a product?

                                        (5 marks)

         (ii) In the last 3 months the manufacturer of skateboards has noticed a decline in sales. What strategy could be adopted to reverse this trend?   **(4 marks)**

3. (a) Outline the characteristics which make a problem suitable for the application of a Critical Path Analysis.   **(3 marks)**

  (b) Domingo Plastics is installing a new machine for the moulding of plastic casings for the electronics industry. This machine specialises in the production of medium-sized casings for video recorders, radio/cassette players and CD players. The machine must be installed and ready for use on a large contract in 3 weeks' time (assume a 5-day working week).

The activities involved in the installation are as shown in the table below.

Activity	Must be preceded by	Duration (days)
A	–	2
B	–	4
C	–	8
D	B	2
E	A	6
F	A	5
G	D, F	3
H	E, G	3
I	C	4
J	H, I	1

    (i)   Draw a diagram to represent this project as a CPA network.   **(4 marks)**

    (ii)   Calculate the Total Float and Free Float for each activity. Determine the minimum project duration to show that the deadline can be met.   **(4 marks)**

    (iii)   Owing to increased demand for CD players the contract has been brought forward and the machine must be ready in 12 days' time. State, with reasons, which activities Domingo Plastics should attempt to reduce.   **(2 marks)**

(c)   The Production Manager has suggested reducing activity F (off-site training for the machine operators) by 2 days. Using the network you have drawn,

    (i)   Explain why this suggestion will not reduce the deadline to day 12.   **(2 marks)**

    (ii)   What other reasons might be used to reject the Production Manager's suggestion?   **(2 marks)**

(d)   Domingo Plastics wants to reduce wastage and faulty items to below 0.5% of output. At present inspection is done at the end of the production line. One worker has suggested the use of quality circles.

    (i)   Define this term and explain the advantages of using them to improve quality control.   **(5 marks)**

    (ii)   What other changes could be made to reduce waste and to improve quality?   **(3 marks)**

4.   ZNB Ltd is a small pottery manufacturer specialising in the production of animal figures for the souvenir and collectors market. It has two very successful ranges depicting horses and pigs. The Managing Director is concerned, however, that the firm is not performing as well as last year and she is concerned at the poor sales of the other 6 ranges of animal figures. Some extracts from ZNB's accounts for the last 2 years are given on the next page.

(a)   Calculate for each year:

    (i)   the Profit Margin ratio   **(2 marks)**

    (ii)   the Return on Capital Employed   **(2 marks)**

    (iii)   the Current ratio   **(2 marks)**

    (iv)   the Acid Test ratio   **(2 marks)**

Turn over

Extract from the Profit and Loss accounts

Year to 30 April 1997			Year to 30 April 1998	
£000s	£000s		£000s	£000s
	750	Sales		900
180		Labour	250	
120	(300)	Materials	180	(430)
	450			470
		Overheads		
80		Production	70	
30		Admin.	60	
50		Sales	110	
40	(200)	Depreciation	30	(270)
	250	Net Profit before tax		200

Extracts from Balance Sheet at:	30/4/97	30/4/98
	£000s	£000s
Net Assets	1290	1330
Fixed Assets	980	900
Current Assets		
Stock	150	250
Debtors	200	450
Cash	120	30
Current Liabilities	160	300

(b) Using the ratios you have calculated and the information in the extracts from the accounts, write a brief report to the Managing Director in a suitable format on the per-formance of ZNB Ltd over the 2 years. Deal with profitability, efficiency and financial status. Mention any other areas of concern that you might have about ZNB's situation. **(10 marks)**

(c) ZNB Ltd is considering the use of a market research company to investigate the current and future market for animal figures. Comment on the advantages and disadvantages of commissioning a primary data research exercise. **(7 marks)**

5. Gregory's is a successful high-street fashion house that is wanting to expand its business over the next 5 years. The company is considering two options. Option A involves the purchase for £400,000 of the adjoining empty shop to make a larger retail outlet for its own branded clothing. The cash flows associated with this option are given below. Option B involves the purchase of a similar fashion retailer in a nearby town for £850,000. This would entail spending £100,000 initially to convert it to the Gregory's style. Cash flows are estimated to be £250,000 in the first year rising by £50,000 p.a. in each of the next 4 years.

Option A

Year	Cash flow (£000s)
0	−400
1	+100
2	+140
3	+180
4	+210
5	+230

(a)   (i)   Construct a table of cash flows for Option B for the 5-year period.   **(3 marks)**

(ii)   Calculate the payback and the NPV for both Option A and Option B (assume a cost of capital of 10%).   **(9 marks)**

No. of years	Discount factor at 10%
0	1.00
1	0.91
2	0.83
3	0.75
4	0.68
5	0.62

(iii)   Discuss the limitations of the investment appraisal technique used.   **(3 marks)**

(b)   Gregory's specialises in the luxury end of the fashion market. What other economic and market factors should it consider before choosing between the two options?   **(10 marks)**

6.   Zulu Enterprises imports African curios for distribution to wholesalers specialising in supplying the art and craft market. Against an uncertain economic background Zulu Enterprises wishes to forecast sales for the middle of 1998. The sales data for the past few years are given in the table overleaf.

Year	Quarter	Sales revenue (£000s)	Centred moving average	Seasonal variation
1995	1	100		
	2	105		
	3	120	109.38	10.62
	4	110	110.63	−0.63
1996	1	105	113.75	−8.75
	2	110	117.50	−7.50
	3	140	119.38	20.62
	4	120	121.88	−1.88
1997	1	110	126.25	−16.22
	2	125	130.00	−5.00
	3	160		
	4	130		
1998	1	120		

(a)   Using the table:

(i)   Calculate the trend figure and the seasonal variation for 1997 Quarter 3, showing all workings.   **(4 marks)**

(ii)   Calculate the average seasonal variation for each quarter.   **(2 marks)**

(iii)   Using graph paper, attempt a forecast of the sales revenue of Zulu Enterprises for Quarter 3 and Quarter 4 of 1998.   **(6 marks)**

(iv)   Explain the shortcomings of the technique used in part (iii).   **(3 marks)**

Turn over

(b)   (i)   Explain **two** advantages and **two** disadvantages of the current distribution channel used by Zulu Enterprises.   **(4 marks)**

      (ii)   What would be the marketing and financial implications of changing the distribution channel to one dealing directly with the retail outlets?   **(6 marks)**

Total: 100 marks

Longman
Examination Board

General Certificate of Education

Business Studies Advanced

Paper 1

Part 2

Time: 2 hours

Instructions

■ Answer **all** the questions in Paper 1, Part 2.

■ Answer questions on separate ruled paper.

Information for candidates

■ You are allowed 2 hours for Paper 1, Part 2

■ The marks available are shown in brackets after each question.

■ The maximum mark for Paper 1, Part 2 is 100.

Topic	Number	Mark
Objectives & the business environment	1.	
	2.	
	3.	
	4.	
	5.	
Marketing	1.	
	2.	
	3.	
	4.	
	5.	
	6.	
Accounting & finance	1.	
	2.	
	3.	
	4.	
	5.	
	6.	
Human resources	1.	
	2.	
	3.	
	4.	
	5.	
Operations management	1.	
	2.	
	3.	
	4.	
	5.	
	Total	

Objectives and the business environment

1. Successive governments have had a policy of reducing direct taxes in order to improve employee motivation. Explain the reasoning behind this policy. **(3 marks)**

2. What is a small firm? State three reasons why small firms exist. **(5 marks)**

3. Why are changes in the structure of the population of interest to business organisations? **(4 marks)**

4. Explain why organisations can sometimes charge the public different prices for the same product or service. **(5 marks)**

5. Give three reasons why organisations need to have clear objectives. **(3 marks)**

Marketing

1. Explain two pricing strategies that a firm introducing an entirely new product to the market could adopt. **(5 marks)**

2. What are the main functions of packaging ? **(4 marks)**

3. Why do firms try to forecast the demand for their products? **(4 marks)**

Turn over

4. Using examples, distinguish between an industrial and a commercial good. **(2 marks)**

5. Explain the term 'moving average'. **(3 marks)**

6. Explain what is meant by the term 'extension strategy' in the product life cycle. **(2 marks)**

Accounting and finance

1. Briefly expain why profit is important to a business. **(6 marks)**

2. Explain when the 'pay back period' method of assessing investment projects might be used. **(4 marks)**

3. Published financial accounts strike a delicate balance between the shareholders' need for openness and the firm's need for secrecy. Explain what you understand by this statement. **(3 marks)**

4. Distinguish between 'fixed' and 'variable' costs. **(3 marks)**

5. Show the formula for calculating the Return on Capital Employed. **(2 marks)**

6. Explain the term 'depreciation'. **(2 marks)**

Human resources

1. Distinguish between 'line' and 'staff' relationships within an organisation. **(4 marks)**

2. Why is the 'span of control' important in any discussion of management style? **(4 marks)**

3. Identify four constraints on trade union power. **(3 marks)**

4. How does job enrichment contribute to motivation? **(3 marks)**

5. Outline three possible barriers to communication in an organisation with a hierarchical structure. **(6 marks)**

Operations management

1. What are the advantages of batch production over job production? **(4 marks)**

2. Explain two objectives of stock management. **(4 marks)**

3. State the formula for calculating the Economic Order Quantity. **(2 marks)**

4. Explain what is meant by 'CAD/CAM'. **(4 marks)**

5. Discuss the possible effects of lean manufacturing on a firm's

    (a) suppliers **(3 marks)**

    (b) workforce **(3 marks)**

Total: 100 marks

Longman Examination Board

General Certificate of Education

Business Studies Advanced

Paper 1

Part 3

Time: 3 hours

Section	Number	Mark
A	1.	
	2.	
	3.	
	4.	
	5.	
	6.	
B	1.	
	2.	
	Total	

Instructions

■ Paper 1, Part 3, has 2 sections, A and B.
  Answer **all** questions in Section A.
  Answer 1 question only in Section B.

■ Answer questions on separate ruled paper.

■ Show all stages in any calculation, and state the units.

■ Where diagrams are required, make sure they are drawn and labelled clearly.

Information for candidates

■ You are allowed 3 hours for Paper 1, Part 3.

■ The marks available are shown in brackets after each question or part-question.

■ Section A has a maximum mark of 80.

■ Section B has a maximum mark of 20.

■ The maximum mark for Paper 1, Part 3, is 100.

Case Study Morrow Brothers (Stationery Supplies) Ltd

This is a third-generation family firm, a limited company, now run by two brothers – Mark and
John Morrow. Mark concentrates on production operations and John, the office and administration.
MBL, as the firm is often called, employs 150 people. It has a turnover of £5.0 million and net profits
of £200,000. The two brothers hold 65% of the shares, with the balance of shares being held by a
venture capitalist.   5

The firm operates from a factory in south London. All its workforce live in the locality and the
majority have been with the firm for many years. Although there is little unemployment in the area the
firm has never had to advertise for production or office staff. All job opportunities are filled through
the recommendation of existing employees. The brothers believe that the firm has functioned like one
big happy family. Their management style is best described as paternalistic.   10

Despite some complaints in the neighbourhood regarding the noise of the machinery and delivery
lorries blocking busy roads at peak times, MBL enjoys a good reputation as a socially responsible
firm. Its employees earn high wages through a group productivity bonus scheme which is designed to
minimise paper waste and machine downtime.   14

Turn over

The firm is part of the UK's fifth largest manufacturing sector which accounts for 7% of UK manufacturing output. The industry has 165,000 employees in some 10,000 companies. Whilst the industry is dominated by a few large firms there are a very large number of small firms operating within a very limited geographic area. The SIA or Stationery Industry Association states that the typical firm employs less than 20 workers, has turnover per employee of £71,000 and profits per employee of £2,500. In 1998 a typical firm works on a profit margin of 3.7%, though this is considerably better than the 1.2 % profit margin recorded in 1994! Competition is intense and where undifferentiated products are concerned a price elasticity of demand of 3 exists.　22

MBL's main business is the production of basic stationery supplies which it sells through wholesalers. Fixed costs, covering selling, administration and production overheads, are currently £800,000. Direct costs for stationery packs are £2.50 for labour and £5.50 for materials. Each pack sells for £10.00. The company is more than breaking even with a reasonable margin of safety.　26

Despite competition, the brothers have found that they have been able to sell all that they produced. Little in the way of marketing has been undertaken with items being routinely made and put into stock. The brothers have put their success down to their keen prices, committed workforce and an ability to supply on demand from stock.　30

The ability to price competitively is due primarily to the firm's continued investment in 'state of the art' machinery. Manual setting and operation of the machinery by the production operatives is a thing of the past. The new machines are fully computerised (CAD/CAM) and operated by employees with specialist knowledge of electronic systems. As a result, productivity has doubled in the last decade. The changes in the nature of their work has caused considerable unrest amongst employees in the last 5 years even though the firm has been willing to spend considerable amounts of money retraining the workforce and has guaranteed no redundancies.　37

Unrest has also been caused by the purchase of paper from Russia rather than Canada. The decision was taken on the grounds of cost. Unfortunately, the paper, which is rather softer, tends to tear more easily in the production process. This has led to several machine shutdowns and the loss of production. The consequent loss of bonus payments to the employees may have caused the recent rise in labour turnover.　42

The cyclical nature of MBL's business has caused problems for both production and inventory control. Business peaks dramatically in September at the start of the school year and in April at the beginning of many companies' financial year. Rather than lay employees on and off, the firm, in recent years, has adjusted to its pattern of demand through the use of short-time and overtime working as well as producing for stock.　47

In the last 2 years the brothers have noted that competition has become more intense. Their profit margins, always slightly better than the industry average, have been squeezed and stock levels have increased. This has caused them to review the situation.　50

John is of the opinion that they have been too reluctant to 'get out and sell their products' in the past. He believes that Morrow Brothers should begin to sell directly to the retail outlets. Last year a marketing consultant was engaged who calculated that such a move would result in sales being reduced initially by 10%. Increased distribution expenses would result in fixed costs rising from £800,000 to £900,000. In the longer term it would be expected that the sales representatives would develop new markets.　56

Mark does not dispute the consultant's figures but believes the market is changing rapidly. He feels that the brothers need to have much more information on the market and its customers in order to make the correct decision. He suspects that the firm needs to redefine its core objective of supplying basic printing materials at a competitive price. Nevertheless, he is certain that it will be necessary to become more competitive in the future in order to survive.　61

The situation facing the brothers is made more complicated by the fact that they have been approached by the owner of another printing firm offering to let them buy it. David Wilson is 68. His son, who was to take over the firm, died in a car crash 5 years ago. Since that time he has lost interest in the firm and now wishes to retire. The firm, Wilson's Ltd, which specialises in producing company literature and promotional material, operates from premises just 4 miles away from Morrow Brothers. The brothers have received the financial information set out in Appendix 1.　67

They believe, however, that the accounts do not give the complete picture. For example, they know that the very large salary Mr Wilson has been drawing from the firm has alienated many of his staff who feel that their contribution to the success of the firm has not been recognised.
No decisions have yet been made but the brothers feel that time is running out.   71

Appendix 1

Wilson's Ltd Balance Sheet as at 31 May 1998

	£ £000s	£ £000s
Fixed assets		
Land and buildings	5 000	
Vehicles	300	
		5 300
Current assets		
Stocks	1 000	
Debtors	850	
Cash	50	
		1 900
Current liabilities		
creditors	1 000	
overdraft	950	1 950
Net current assets		(50)
Net assets		(5 250)
Shareholders' funds		
Ordinary share capital	1 500	
Reserves	3 750	5 250

During the year ending May 1998, Sales were £10 million and Purchases were £5 million. Interest paid on the overdraft was £102,000 and profit before tax and interest (PBIT) was £200,000. Opening and closing stock was £1 million. Land and buildings were revalued by £1.5 million in 1995.

Ratios for the last 5 years are as follows:

	1993	1994	1995	1996	1997
Profit margin	8	6	4	3	2
Net asset turnover	6.2	5.9	4.1	3.9	1.9
Debtors turnover	8.3	9.6	11.4	11.5	11.8
Stock turnover	7.1	7.3	8.4	9.1	10.0
Current ratio	2.1	1.9	1.8	1.4	0.98
Acid test	1.3	1.1	1.0	1.1	0.46

Section A
Answer **all** questions.

1. Briefly explain the following terms as used in the text:

    (a) limited company (line 1)   **(2 marks)**

    (b) venture capitalist (line 5)   **(2 marks)**

    (c) price elasticity of demand (line 22)   **(2 marks)**

    (d) productivity (line 34)   **(2 marks)**

    (e) core objective (line 59).   **(2 marks)**

                                                                        Turn over

2. (a) Calculate for Morrow Brothers Ltd:

     (i) the contribution per unit   **(2 marks)**

     (ii) the break-even output   **(2 marks)**

     (iii) the margin of safety.   **(2 marks)**

   (b) Based on the findings of the consultant (line 53) what would be the new margin of safety? **(4 marks)**

3. The future success of the firm may depend on the decisions which the owners of MBL are about to take. Analyse and evaluate the factors you think should be considered before the decision is taken to sell direct to retailers. **(15 marks)**

4. (a) What do you understand by the term 'paternalistic' management style (line 10)? **(5 marks)**

   (b) Assess the logic of Morrow Brothers Ltd's policy of appointing staff on the basis of recommendation of existing employees. **(10 marks)**

5. To what extent do you believe that it would have been possible for MBL to have avoided unrest amongst the employees during the recent period of change? **(10 marks)**

6. (a) On the basis of the information given in Appendix 1, assess the financial position of Wilson's Ltd from 1993 to 1998. **(15 marks)**

   (b) Comment on the limitations of your conclusions. **(5 marks)**

Section B
Answer **either** Question 1 **or** Question 2.

1. Many people have voiced concern at Directors in a company giving themselves large increases in pay whilst imposing severe pay restraints on their employees.

   Discuss why a firm might pursue such policies. **(20 marks)**

or

2. (a) With the aid of examples, explain what you understand by the term 'social responsibility' and why it is desirable. **(8 marks)**

   (b) How effective are the ways in which society can encourage firms to become more socially responsible? **(12 marks)**

Total: 100 marks

Longman
Examination Board

Number	Mark
1.	
2.	
3.	
4.	
5.	
6.	
Total:	

General Certificate of Education

Business Studies Advanced

Paper 2

Part 1

Time: 3 hours

Instructions

■ Paper 2, Part 1, has 6 questions. **Answer 4 questions only.**

■ Answer questions on separate ruled paper.

■ Show all stages in any calculation, and state the units.

■ Where diagrams are required, make sure they are drawn and labelled clearly.

Information for candidates

■ You are allowed 3 hours for Paper 2, Part 1.

■ The marks available are shown in brackets after each question or part-question.

■ The maximum mark for Paper 2, Part 1, is 100.

---

1. Study the information below and answer all parts of the question which follow.

B.J. Amin's summarised Profit and Loss Accounts 1997–1998		
	1997	1998
	£000s	£000s
Sales turnover	21,600	25,624
Gross profit	7,200	8,007
Operating profit	3,240	4,612

B.J. Amin's summarised Balance Sheet 1997–1998 (as at 30 September 1998)		
	1997	1998
	£000s	£000s
Fixed assets	10,218	12,300
Stock	3,218	5,812
Debtors	2,219	3,450
Cash	324	565
Current liabilities	(4,522)	(5,862)
Working capital	1,239	3,965
Net assets	11,457	16,265
Long-term liabilities	5,860	2,724
Share capital	2,086	9,086
Reserves	3,511	4,455
Capital employed	11,457	16,265

Turn over

(a) State **two** ratios that a bank manager might use when considering the request for a loan from B.J. Amin. Give a reason for the choice of each ratio. **(4 marks)**

(b) Evaluate the profitability and financial status of B.J. Amin between 1997 and 1998 with the help of appropriate ratios. **(10 marks)**

(c) State **two** limitations of using the 1998 ratios as a guide to the future performance of B.J. Amin. **(3 marks)**

(d) B.J. Amin is a national chain of retail outlets. The company has decided to introduce bar coding and scanning at all of the tills linked to a central computer at its head-quarters in Wakefield. Discuss how this might affect the firm in the future. **(8 marks)**

2. La Hacienda is a small British-owned hotel in southern Spain that specialises in gourmet holidays for vegetarians. Initial success in its first few years has encouraged the owner Mr Hones to increase the number of rooms with the addition of a new extension. This must be completed in time for the arrival of a large party of American guests in 90 days' time. The initial foundation work was completed earlier in the year but Mr Hones is concerned about the progress of the builders, Lento Construction. He held a meeting with the site manager who provided a breakdown of the tasks involved, their likely duration and the order of completion, as shown in the table below.

Activity label	Activity	Duration (days)
A	Building of walls	36
B	Landscaping	14
C	Roof construction	10
D	Interior plastering	18
E	Fitting of doors and windows	4
F	Plumbing	14
G	Exterior painting	10
H	Interior painting	15
I	Soft furnishing	6
J	Certification by Spanish Tourist Board	2

(a) Draw a network diagram based on the above, given that:

Activity	Preceded by
A is the start of the project	—
B and C	A
E and G	C
D and F	E
H	D
I	H and F
J is the final activity	

(7 marks)

(b)   Determine the critical path and the project duration. Can the extension be completed in time for the arrival of the American party? **(5 marks)**

(c)   To allow for staff training in the new extension Mr Hones wants to reduce the project time by 3 days. Some of the activities can be reduced by employing extra labour but this will add to the cost of the project. Suggest which activities should be chosen if costs are to be kept to a minimum. No single activity can be reduced by more than 1 day.

Activity	Cost to reduce by 1 day (£)
A	80
C	70
G	40
B	50
H	60

Give reasons for your choice of activities and state the total cost. **(5 marks)**

(d)   At the moment all of La Hacienda's records and systems are done manually on paper. Outline two applications of IT to a hotel and state the benefits each can achieve.

(8 marks)

3.   Design Mouldings produces deluxe padded chairs for large hotels and conference centres. It sells these direct to the end users at a price of £26 per chair. The projected output for next year is 180,000 units though it has a capacity with its existing machinery to make 200,000 units. Fixed costs at its Leeds plant are £4.40 per chair at full capacity. Material costs are £9 per chair, labour costs are £2 per unit and other variable costs are £4.

A French company that specialises in organising Europe-wide conferences has offered Design Mouldings a special order for 20,000 chairs. This is the largest single order ever received but the French company only wants to pay £17 per chair. It also wants its own brand name on each chair which will cost 60p per unit. Some minor changes to the design will add a further £28,000 to the cost of the order.

The management of Design Mouldings is divided on the issue as acceptance of the order would mean postponing the launch of a new venture. The Development Director Mike Jones wanted to manufacture a basic plastic chair targeted at schools, colleges and other lower-budget customers.

(a)   (i)   Calculate Design Mouldings' break-even level of output. **(4 marks)**

       (ii)   Calculate its margin of safety. **(2 marks)**

(b)   With reference to the special order:

       (i)   On numerical grounds only, should Design Mouldings accept this special order? Explain your answer. **(4 marks)**

       (ii)   Analyse the non-numerical factors that Design Mouldings should take into account when making this decision. **(7 marks)**

(c)   If Design Mouldings rejected the order and decided to adopt Mike Jones' suggestion, what pricing policy would you recommend the firm to follow? Give reasons for your answer.

(8 marks)

4.   **Deserved pay rises or just Fat Cats?**
In 1994 the details of basic pay packages, share options and other benefits for the former nationalised industry bosses became public knowledge (see table below). These increases caused uproar in the media, indignation among the general public and outrage from the trade unions.

Turn over

David Stirzaker, a senior official of Unison, Britain's largest union, said his members working at British Gas had received less than 3% last year in comparison with the 75% annual pay rise awarded to Cedric Brown, the chief executive.

Earnings of Chief Executives

	1981 (£)	1994 (£)	% change
Telecommunications	57,650	465,000	707
Gas	48,255	475,000	884
Electricity	44,731	293,750	557
Water supply	27,188	250,000	820

The utilities responded to the media outcry and questions from MPs by insisting that the newly privatised companies had to 'recruit, retain and motivate top calibre management', if they were to expand internationally and to compete successfully with other British-based international companies. They further defended the salaries by pointing out that they were set by remuneration committees made up of non-executive directors.

In response to the public outcry the government appointed Sir Richard Greensbury, Chairman of Marks and Spencer, to prepare a code of conduct for executive pay.

Meanwhile in the highly competitive food retail sector Archie Norman, chief executive of Asda, was making a £1.26m profit by exercising share options granted when he joined the company. These were a reward for transforming Asda from a £1bn debt-ridden company to the third largest food retailer. Under Norman's management profits rose from £183m to £246.2m and sales from £5.3bn to £5.7bn in four years from 1991. In the same period Asda shares rose from 23p to 94p. Archie Norman could justifiably claim he deserved his remuneration package as all of the stakeholders in Asda had benefited under his guidance. More than half of the workforce are beneficiaries of a company share option scheme.

(a) Apart from shareholders and employees, give two other examples of stakeholders in a business such as Asda. **(2 marks)**

(b) 'All employees should be paid what they are worth.' To what extent do you agree with this view in relation to the pay of Unison's members on the shopfloor of the former nationalised industries compared with the pay of the Chief Executives? **(8 marks)**

(c) Asda use a share option scheme for all of its employees.

   (i) Explain how such a scheme works. **(4 marks)**

   (ii) Comment on the attitude of workers to such a scheme. **(3 marks)**

(d) Consider whether it is appropriate for governments to intervene in business decision-making. **(8 marks)**

5. **Tea Drinkers No More!**

Cold drinks have taken over from tea as the UK's favourite drink. In 1996 it is estimated that consumers drank 8 billion litres of tea but over 10 billion litres of soft drinks. This trend is set to continue as Coca-Cola believes that the UK is still an immature market with consumers drinking on average only 150 cans of fizzy drink per year compared to the 300 cans per year in the US. The UK cola market is worth a staggering £6bn. It is dominated by Coke and Pepsi although recently it has faced competition from supermarket own brands and Virgin Cola (see table).

UK Market Share

	%
Coke/Pepsi	78
Own Label	14
Virgin cola	4
Other brands	4

The impact of Virgin Cola

In October 1994 Virgin launched its cola drink with an exclusive deal with Tesco and were able to capture 6% of supermarket sales. Cola sales in supermarkets account for 56% of the total market, the rest being sold through small retailers and vending machines. Virgin opted for the Tesco deal so as to minimise marketing costs and to keep distribution simple with large deliveries to central locations. Virgin Cola was helped enormously by using the Virgin brand name and by the 'free' publicity the so-called 'cola war' generated. Branson ensured plenty of media coverage with his claim that Coke and Pepsi were charging a higher price or 'Brand Tax' to pay for their expensive and exhaustive advertising campaigns.

The response of Coke and Pepsi

Coke responded not by matching Virgin's price cuts but with a £40m advertising campaign that stressed its product as the 'real thing'. Coke were not overly concerned because they believed that the UK market still had plenty of potential for growth and that Virgin could not challenge Coke's supremacy in the small retail sector. In this area Coke and Pepsi between them control over 94% of the market. They believe that the much higher cost of establishing a national distribution and service network is beyond Virgin's capability.

On the larger market Pepsi have launched a world-wide advertising campaign. The £500m 'Project Blue' aims to differentiate Pepsi from its main rival Coke, and other brands such as Virgin Cola, by changing the colour of the Pepsi can to electric blue. Coke meanwhile has used its considerably larger financial resources to invest heavily in the emerging markets. Investment in the early 1990s in Eastern Europe alone amounted to over £1.5bn.

(a)   With reference to the article, explain the following terms:

    (i)   'brand names'   **(2 marks)**

    (ii)   'immature market'   **(2 marks)**

    (iii)   'own brand'.   **(2 marks)**

(b)   Calculate the annual value of cola sales for:

    (i)   Coca-Cola/Pepsi   **(1 mark)**

    (ii)   Virgin Cola.   **(1 mark)**

(c)   Considering the various marketing strategies available, explain why:

    (i)   Virgin might choose a strategy that concentrates on price and place,   **(8 marks)**

    (ii)   Coke and Pepsi might stress promotion.   **(5 marks)**

(d)   Explain why Coke and Pepsi may not feel threatened by own label products and the emergence of Virgin Cola.   **(4 marks)**

6.   **'To move or not to move, that is the question!'**

Suzanne Gregory owns a well-established sports shop in a town centre in the north of England. She is considering relocating to a new development that is being built 10 miles away on the outskirts of the town. The new complex involves 20 different specialist retail outlets to be built between a hypermarket and a privately run leisure centre.

Suzanne believes that if she moves there is a 50% chance that her net income will increase by £280,000, a 30% chance it will remain unchanged and a 20% chance it will fall by £120,000. The alternative is to remain in the town centre and hope that the council's 'free car parking' scheme will attract customers from further away. Suzanne has estimated that if the council's visitor projections are correct there is a 60% chance her overall net income will rise by £160,000 and a 40% chance it will fall by £30,000.

To complicate matters further none of her current staff, who have been with her since the start, own a car. They would all find it more costly and more inconvenient to travel out to the new complex. For most of the staff who live on the other side of town it would mean an extra 30 minutes' travel time in each direction. Four of the staff have already indicated that they would not be available if the shop moved to the new site. This would result in Suzanne having to

Turn over

train new staff. Suzanne believes that her knowledgeable and friendly staff together with the wide range of reasonably priced goods were her unique selling points.

(a) (i) Outline the circumstances in which decision trees are useful as an aid to decision-making. **(2 marks)**

(ii) Explain how the actual value of the different outcomes might have been calculated. **(2 marks)**

(iii) 'Explain what is meant by the terms 'expected monetary value' and 'unique selling point'. **(4 marks)**

(b) Set out Suzanne's problem in the form of a decision tree indicating the probabilities and actual values. Calculate the expected monetary values. What is the optimal decision on this basis? **(6 marks)**

(c) How might Suzanne overcome the human resource problem presented by the relocation? **(5 marks)**

(d) To relocate Suzanne will require extra finance of £150,000 to pay for new fixtures and fittings and to fund the additional stock to meet the estimated demand. Considering that she is a sole trader, suggest, with reasons, **two** sources of finance that Suzanne could use. **(6 marks)**

Total: 100 marks

Longman
Examination Board

General Certificate of Education

Business Studies Advanced

Paper 2

Part 2

Time: 2 hours

Instructions

■ Answer **all** the questions in Paper 2, Part 2.

■ Answer questions on separate ruled paper.

Information for candidates

■ You are allowed 2 hours for Paper 2, Part 2.

■ The marks available are shown in brackets after each question.

■ The maximum mark for Paper 2, Part 2 is 100.

Topic	Number	Mark
Objectives & the business environment	1.	
	2.	
	3.	
	4.	
	5.	
Marketing	1.	
	2.	
	3.	
	4.	
	5.	
	6.	
Accounting & finance	1.	
	2.	
	3.	
	4.	
	5.	
Human resources	1.	
	2.	
	3.	
	4.	
	5.	
Operations management	1.	
	2.	
	3.	
	4.	
	5.	
Total		

Objectives and the business environment

1. Outline the implications for manufacturers of a rise in the exchange rate for sterling.
   (4 marks)

2. Distinguish between 'opportunity cost' and 'social cost'. **(4 marks)**

3. Identify four groups that could be considered as stakeholders of a registered charity such as Oxfam. **(2 marks)**

4. What are the main functions of a business plan? **(6 marks)**

5. Outline four economies of scale which a firm may obtain by increasing the scale of its operations. **(4 marks)**

Marketing

1. Give two reasons why a firm, for a limited period, may sell part of its product line at a loss.
   (4 marks)

2. State **two** ways of segmenting the market for motor cars. **(2 marks)**

Turn over

3. How might an organisation measure the effectiveness of its advertising? **(4 marks)**

4. State two ways in which the relationship between production and marketing might change as a firm becomes more marketing orientated. **(4 marks)**

5. State four purposes of branding. **(4 marks)**

6. Give two reasons why sampling may provide inaccurate information. **(4 marks)**

Accounting and finance

1. Distinguish between 'contribution' and 'profit'. **(3 marks)**

2. Using an example, what do you understand by the term 'matching principle'? **(3 marks)**

3. Identify four potential sources of finance for an individual starting his or her own business. **(4 marks)**

4. Show how a liquidity ratio is calculated and explain its use. **(5 marks)**

5. State two functions of a budgetary system within an organisation. **(2 marks)**

Human resources

1. Distinguish between a 'formal group' and an 'informal group' in an organisation. **(4 marks)**

2. Identify three types of action which may be taken by employees in a dispute with their employer. **(3 marks)**

3. Give two actions that a Human Resources Department might take as a result of a policy to expand into overseas markets. **(4 marks)**

4. State three benefits to a firm from pursuing a policy of delegation. **(3 marks)**

5. Comment on the leadership styles most likely to be effective in:

    (a) the armed forces **(3 marks)**

    (b) a research team within a pharmaceutical firm. **(3 marks)**

Operations management

1. How might benchmarking help an organisation to improve its productivity? **(4 marks)**

2. How might new technology hinder the performance of a business? **(5 marks)**

3. State three factors that might affect the decision of a firm as to where to locate a new factory. **(3 marks)**

4. What difficulties might a firm face when changing to a system of automated production? **(3 marks)**

5. How might Critical Path Analysis be useful when undertaking Just In Time production? **(6 marks)**

Turn over

Total: 100 marks

Longman Examination Board

General Certificate of Education

Business Studies Advanced

Paper 2

Part 3

Time: 3 hours

Section	Number	Mark
A		
B	1.	
	2.	
	3.	
	4.	
	5.	
	6.	
	Total	

Instructions

- Paper 2, Part 3, has 2 sections, A and B.
  Answer **all** questions in Section A.
  Answer 2 questions only in Section B.

- Answer questions on separate ruled paper.

- Show all stages in any calculation, and state the units.

- Where diagrams are required, make sure they are drawn and labelled clearly.

Information for candidates

- You are allowed 3 hours for Paper 2, Part 3.

- The marks available are shown in brackets after each question or part-question.

- Section A has a maximum mark of 50.

- Section B has a maximum mark of 50.

- The maximum mark for Paper 2, Part 3, is 100.

Case study   Babywear Limited

Babywear Limited, a family owned company, is a leading manufacturer of baby clothes with annual sales of around £100 million. The firm produces branded goods which are distributed to all leading retailers throughout the British Isles. It is the seventh biggest producer of branded goods with 5% of the market. The UK concentration ratio for the top 5 firms in the industry is 42% in 1998 down from 49% in 1988. There are over 60 British manufacturers, many of whom are small and producing for local or niche markets. Baby clothes are also imported from the continent –particularly the low-cost producers of Eastern Europe.

The firm was started by David Singh, a textiles machinery engineer, in 1963. During its early years the firm experienced rapid growth in bouyant market conditions. At this time much of the output was produced to the specification of several large multiple stores. By 1975 though, increasing pressure on profit margins (caused by these retailers demanding cost reductions) convinced David to develop his own range of high-quality branded children's clothing. This coincided with the opening of the second factory. A third factory was opened in 1984 when Marcus Singh, the son of David, joined the firm. The firm has always managed to make a profit and apart from a disasterous period when they tried to break into the European market there has been a steady growth in profits.

Turn over

The company operates on 3 sites in Yorkshire – an area of high unemployment. The longest-established site in Barnsley (attached to the Head Office) has little room for expansion. It is a prime site for sale and redevelopment. The factories in Wakefield and Rotherham provide three-quarters of total output and there is room for expansion. All sites operate on a batch production process.

The company brandname 'Babywear' has been used by the firm for over 25 years. It is held in high regard by the consumers. Maintaining the reputation of the brand is seen by David and Marcus as the key to sales growth and profitability. Nevertheless, they are becoming increasingly concerned about the growth of 'own brands' in the 1990s. Own brand goods are often 20% cheaper than the comparable branded good, even though they are often almost identical in terms of material and styling.

The lower store price for non-branded goods arises partly because of long-run economies in the production process but also because the retail chains tend to spend far less per unit of sales on advertising and promotion. In comparison Babywear spends roughly 12% of its turnover on sales promotion. 50% of this will be spent on direct consumer advertising with the rest split between trade promotions (35%) and consumer promotions (e.g. competitions and money-off offers).

Babywear has recently been approached by a leading retailer, Pricerite, and asked to produce a small range of children's clothing under the chain's label. In the first year, output under this contract would be worth a minimum of £10 million, but this (according to Pricerite) could easily double in future years. Although the contract would require the purchase of new and more sophisticated line machinery, Marcus estimates that, within 5 years, this could be paid for out of the extra profits they would earn. In the first instance the agreement would be for 5 years and would require anything between 10% and 25% of Babywear's current productive capacity. Cost increases based on future inflation rates are built into the contract.

The problem facing the firm has also been compounded by another factor. Babywear has just written to all its customers informing them of a 3% across-the-range increase in the price of its products. This is less than the current rate of inflation. However, one particular retailer, Tots and Toddlers, with a chain of shops across Yorkshire and Lancashire has written complaining about the price increase. The letter also suggested that Babywear's marketing strategy was wrong. In particular, the amount spent on direct advertising was excessive and resulted in higher prices to retailers and consumers. Mrs Jones, Managing Director of Tots and Toddlers, argued that much of this could be used in trade promotions encouraging independent retailers and specialist chains of children's shops to stock Babywear products. These firms would then be more competitive when compared with other retailers who stocked own brand baby goods.

Marcus wishes to go ahead with Pricerite's proposed contract. David, however, is not convinced that the proposal is in the best interests of the company. In particular he points to the 8% profit margin which is considerably lower than that currently earned by the firm. He believes that, in the long run, better opportunities may be offered in other segments of the clothing market. In the short run, though, he believes it may be better to consider rationalising production by closing the Barnsley factory.

The Directors of Babywear have the following information available to them in considering the situation they face:

Appendix 1   Financial information

Babywear Ltd
Profit and Loss Account for years ending

	30.12.97	30.12.96
	£m	£m
Turnover	106	101
Profit before tax	23	26
Tax	9	10
Net profit	14	16
Dividends	3	4
Retained profit	11	12

Babywear Ltd
Balance Sheet as at

	30.12.97			30.12.96		
	£m	£m	£m	£m	£m	£m
Fixed assets			121			101
Current assets						
Stocks	110			58		
Debtors	70			65		
Cash	30			49		
		210			172	
Current liabilities						
Short-term loans	20			10		
Creditors	140			103		
		(160)			(113)	
Net current assets			50			59
Net assets			171			160
Capital and reserves						
Owners capital	30			30		
Reserves	125			114		
Equity share-holders funds		155			144	
Long-term liabilities		16			16	
Capital employed			171			160

Appendix 2   Other statistical information

Item 1
Summary of results from a recently completed market research survey into the general baby-wear market
% of respondants replying that the following factors were 'important' or 'very important'

Factor	%
Styling	50
Quality of fabric	35
Recommendation by washing machine manufacturer	45
Recommendation by friend	50
Price	70

Item 2
Index of prices of baby clothing and the RPI

Year	Branded goods	Unbranded goods	RPI
1988	100	100	100
1990	104	98	106
1992	108	102	111
1994	110	105	115
1996	114	108	120
1998	117	110	124

Turn over

Item 3
Size of baby market (live births per annum)
(base year 1988 = 100)

Year	Index of size
1988	100
1990	98
1992	96
1994	94
1996	95
1998	95

Item 4
Sales by retail sector

	1988 %	1998 %
Independent firms	20 (25)	15 (30)
Small chains	40 (40)	35 (40)
Large chains	40 (35)	50 (30)

NB   Babywear sales to each sector are shown in brackets.

Item 5   Production capacity utilisation in baby clothing firms

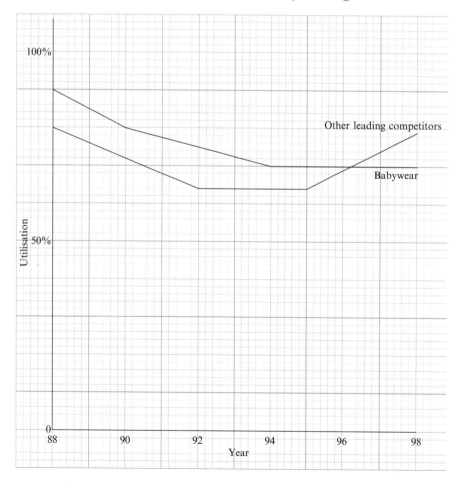

Item 6   Average annual clothing expenditure on children 0–2 years

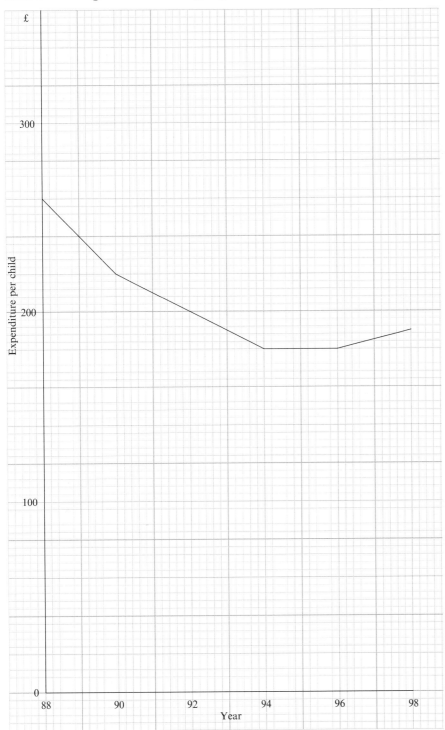

Section A
Answer **all** questions.

David and Marcus have failed to reach agreement on the best course of action open to the company. They have requsted you, a business consultant, to prepare a report for presentation to the Board of Directors. In particular the report should cover:

(a) an assessment of Babywear's current situation

(b) an evaluation of each of the options under discussion.   **(50 marks)**

Turn over

Section B
Answer **two** questions.

1. To what extent does forecasting enable an organisation to make better decisions?

   (25 marks)

2. (a) Explain why so many small firms remain small. **(10 marks)**

   (b) To what extent should the government step in to remedy this problem? **(15 marks)**

3. (a) Discuss what documents an individual should provide to support an application for a bank loan to start up a business. **(10 marks)**

   (b) Comment on the adequacy of these documents to assess an application for a loan.

   (15 marks)

4. (a) Distinguish between job and batch production systems. **(5 marks)**

   (b) How might a bread manufacturer gain from changing production processes from batch to flow? **(10 marks)**

   (c) What problems do you think might arise as a result of such a change? **(10 marks)**

5. Strikes are a thing of the past!

   (a) Discuss this statement. **(10 marks)**

   (b) To what extent does this indicate an improvement in British industrial relations?

   (15 marks)

6. Increasing numbers of people are working from home rather than the office.

   (a) Explain why this has happened. **(10 marks)**

   (b) Assess whether this trend is likely to continue. **(15 marks)**

   Total: 100 marks

Solutions to practice exam papers

1. (a)   (i) $\text{Break-even} = \dfrac{\text{Fixed cost}}{\text{Price} - \text{Variable cost}}$

$$= \frac{£2,000,000}{£5} = 400,000 \text{ units}$$

The margin of safety $=$ Current output $-$ Break-even output

$$= 700,000 \text{ units} - 400,000 \text{ units}$$

$$= 300,000 \text{ units} \hspace{3cm} \textbf{2 marks}$$

(ii) $\text{Price elasticity of demand} = \dfrac{\text{proportional change in demand}}{\text{proportional change in price}}$

$$= \frac{250,000/700,000}{2/9}$$

$$= 1.6$$

The product is price elastic. In other words it is responsive to changes in price. For every 1 percent change in price, demand will change by 1.6 percent.   **3 marks**

> **TIP**
>
> Always give the equations in full before doing the calculation.

(iii)   Price elasticity is useful to Softies Ltd as it shows the likely reaction of consumers to changes in price. This will help better decision-making when the firm reviews its marketing policy, and in particular the type of pricing policy to adopt.

Break-even is also useful as it indicates to Softies how many Giant Pandas need to be sold before a profit can be made on the product. This can be combined with market research to ensure that the market for the toy is sufficient to reach the minimum sales to break even.   **6 marks**

> **TIP**
>
> Note how the answer is related to the case study in question. Ensure that your comments refer to the specific company by name and the product or issue under consideration.

(iv)   Softies imports its products from Taiwan, therefore the exchange rate is very important to the company. If the pound rises in value it means that the imports cost less in the UK which will boost the profit margin. In a similar manner a fall in the value of the pound will squeeze profit margins or cause Softies to raise its UK price. This might result in the toys becoming less competitive and sales falling towards the break-even level. Some insurance against foreign exchange fluctuations can be taken by buying currency on the forward market. This, however, involves a transaction cost that will reduce Softies' profits.   **4 marks**

(b)   (i)   'Batch production' is where a limited number of identical products is made, usually to meet a specific order. At each stage of production the entire batch is processed before being sent onto the next stage. 'Flow production', however, involves the manufacture of an item in a continually moving process from stage to stage, such as in car assembly.   **2 marks**

(ii)   The main advantages are:

- economies of scale, e.g. bulk purchasing discounts
- increased speed and scale of output

■ lower unit costs
■ a more standardised product can be made
■ easier to regulate quality

(1 mark for each relevant advantage) **4 marks**

TIP

These points must be related to the production of toys, especially the Giant Panda.

(iii) HRM problems associated with flow production are:

■ less labour required
■ repetitive and boring manual operations
■ workers on production lines only involved in a small part of job cycle
■ lower worker motivation, therefore higher labour turnover and absenteeism

Softies could approach these problems by:

■ redeployment of excess labour to other functions
■ job enrichment
■ job enlargement
■ encouragement of quality circles
■ creation of teams

(1 mark for an accurate description of the problem and 1 mark for a suitable approach) **4 marks**

2. (a) (i)

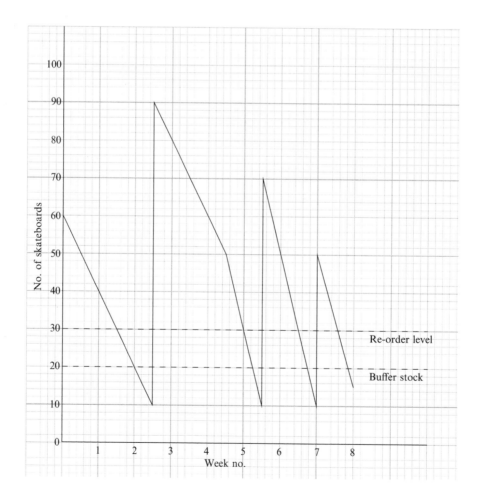

(1 mark for each correct usage line and delivery line) **7 marks**

(ii) Closing stock figure is 15 units **1 mark**

(iii) Unrealistic assumptions include:

- linearity of use of stock
- delivered stock being available immediately
- no damaged or wrongly delivered stock
- re-order level assumes no unpredictable event   **2 marks**

(b) (i) Buffer stock is the desired safety or minimum stock required by a firm just in case some unforeseen event occurs. **(1)**

Cool Sports Ltd would set a buffer stock level depending on:

- the reliability of the supplier
- the anticipated level of demand
- the variability of demand
- the space available for storage
- the finance needed to fund the stocks

(1 mark for each reasonable answer)   **4 marks**

(ii) In week 7, demand was unusually high at 40 units per week.

The last two deliveries before week 8 were below the normal batch quantity, leaving Cool Sports understocked.

(1 mark for each reason)   **2 marks**

(c) (i) The PLC assists a manufacturer by indicating the likely demand for a product which in turn will affect the desired stock-holding level. In the launch stage a manufacturer must be prepared to hold increasing stock levels if a new product is to be launched successfully. Orders received from wholesalers and retailers must be met quickly in order to satisfy an interested market. When a product enters its mature stage a stable stock level is needed to satisfy the steady demand from regular customers. As the product enters the decline stage a manufacturer will want to reduce stock levels so as to avoid unwanted stock that can only be sold at a large discount. At all stages in the PLC the manufacturer has to anticipate market demand.

(1 + 1 marks for identifying correct stock level plus providing an explanation)   **5 marks**

(ii) The life of a product can be increased through the use of 'extension strategies'. The following could assist a manufacturer to revitalise the skateboard market:

- redesigning the product (shape, colour, etc.)
- adding an extra feature
- repositioning its place in the market by altering the price and image, e.g. reducing price in order to capture a younger market
- changing the advertising strategy to appeal to a new additional market, e.g. a foreign market or a female market   **4 marks**

TIP

It is essential that your comments refer to the product in the case study and not to products in general.

3. (a) A problem is suitable for CPA if it has a series of events that are sequential **(1)**, there is a need to minimise time or cost **(1)** and there is a need to use resources effectively **(1)**. A good example would be building a house **(1)** or resurfacing a motorway **(1)**.   **3 marks**

(b) (i)

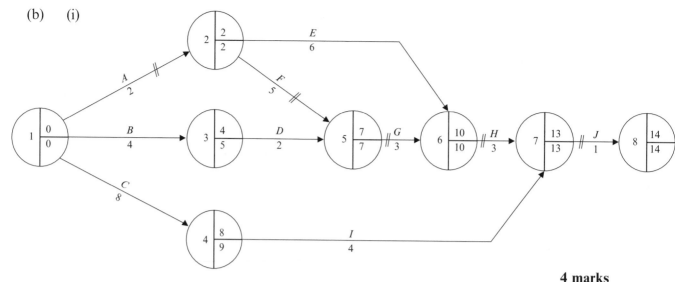

4 marks

(ii)

Activity	Total Float	Free Float
A	0	0
B	1	0
C	1	0
D	1	1
E	2	2
F	0	0
G	0	0
H	0	0
I	1	1
J	0	0

($\frac{1}{2}$ mark deducted from 2 for each incorrect float time in each column)

The project can be completed by the deadline as the duration is only 14 days.

4 marks

(iii) The project can only be shortened by reducing the time taken to complete those activities that are critical **(1)**, that is any of events A, F, G, H, or J **(1)**.   **2 marks**

(c) (i) Although activity F is critical, shortening it by 2 days only affects the project duration by 1 day. This is because the routes BDGHJ and CIJ become new critical paths at 13 days each.   **2 marks**

(ii) Reducing training could have other negative effects, such as:

■ lower productivity
■ increase in waste through incorrect procedures
■ lower motivation of workforce

Any of these could result in the order being completed late.   **2 marks**

(d) (i) A quality circle is a discussion group composed of a wide range of workers, particularly from the factory floor, that meets on a regular basis to discuss quality problems and to recommend solutions.

The advantages of using them are:

■ the factory-floor workers' detailed knowledge of the production process can be harnessed to solve production and quality problems
■ workers appreciate the opportunity to demonstrate their knowledge in a problem solving environment. This is a boost for worker motivation
■ a wider range of solutions is considered
■ it improves consultation and communication within the organisation
■ it is a form of job enrichment

(2 marks for a full definition and 1 + 1 for each point and development)   **5 marks**

TIP

Quality circles are as much about developing good human relations and communications as they are about improving product quality.

(ii) At present the quality is only 'inspected in' at the end of the production process. A better method would be to have continuous quality control **(1)** with the workforce being given the responsibility to 'build in' quality at each production stage **(1)**. The use of simple control charts **(1)** and random sampling **(1)** would highlight problems before they led to rejected items being produced. In financial terms, a bonus for the reduction of waste may be enough to reduce waste caused simply by operator error **(1)**.

3 marks

			1997	1998

4. (a) (i) Profit Margin $= \dfrac{\text{Operating profit}}{\text{Sales}} = \dfrac{250}{750} * 100 = 33.3\%$; $\dfrac{200}{900} * 100 = 22.2\%$

2 marks

(ii) ROCE $= \dfrac{\text{Operating profit}}{\text{Net assets}} = \dfrac{250}{1290} * 100 = 19.4\%$; $\dfrac{200}{1300} * 100 = 15\%$

2 marks

(iii) Current ratio $= \dfrac{\text{Current assets}}{\text{Current liabilities}} = \dfrac{470}{160} = 2.94$; $\dfrac{730}{300} = 2.43$

2 marks

(iv) Acid test $= \dfrac{\text{Current assets} - \text{Stock}}{\text{Current liabilities}} = \dfrac{470-150}{160} = 2$; $\dfrac{730-250}{300} = 1.6$

2 marks

(b) The answer must be in report format with the following or similar headings:

To
From
Date
Subject **(1)**

The report should deal with the following 4 areas:

Profitability
Despite increased sales of £150,000 gross profit has only risen by £20,000 and net profit has fallen by £50,000.
The profit margin has fallen from 33.3% in 1997 to 22.2% in 1998.
ROCE has also fallen from 19.4% to 15%.

Efficiency
Stock turn in days has increased from 73 days to 101 days indicating that resources are not being used as efficiently.
In a similar way the debtor period has lengthened alarmingly from 97 days for collection to 183 days. This is a serious deterioration.

Financial status
The current ratio and acid test ratio appear to be too high. Although this would appear to suggest that the business had adequate resources to meet current debts, it indicates an inefficient use of finance.
Although sales have risen by only 20%, stock has risen by 66.6%, tying up an extra £100,000 of finance.
In a similar way, finance tied up in credit offered to customers has increased 125%.

Other points

Although savings have been made in production overheads the cost of administration and sales has more than doubled. This requires further investigation.

Labour costs have risen 39% in the year. Has this been caused by the employment of extra staff or high pay settlements, or both?

(1 + 1 for each point made and developed up to a maximum of 10. The answer must cover at least 3 sections) **10 marks**

> **TIP**
>
> Look for some obvious problems such as overstocking, growing debtors, lack of cash, rising labour costs, etc. These are commonly used scenarios for exam questions.

(c) The use of a market research company would provide the following:

Advantages:

- expertise in the design and implementation of the data collection
- current, up-to-date information is provided
- primary data is specific to the needs of ZNB Ltd
- may suggest new areas for investigation
- ZNB Ltd can concentrate on production without releasing resources to an area where they lack expertise

Disadvantages:

- cost
- time taken to obtain the data
- the size of the sample that can be afforded (the smaller the size of sample, the less reliable are the findings).

(1 mark for explaining what primary data is and 1 + 1 for each point and development) **7 marks**

> **TIP**
>
> Remember it is often better for a business to concentrate on its core function rather than to use scarce resources attempting to do something it has no expertise in.

5. (a) (i)

Option B

Year	Cash flow (£000s)
0	−950
1	+250
2	+300
3	+350
4	+400
5	+450

3 marks

(ii) Payback:

	Option A		Option B	
Year	Net cash flow (£000s)	Cumulative cash flow	Net cash flow (£000s)	Cumulative cash flow
0	−400	−400	−950	−950
1	+100	−300	+250	−700
2	+140	−160	+300	−400
3	+180	+20	+350	−50
4	+210	+230	+400	+350
5	+230	+460	+450	+800

Payback for Option A occurs in the third year. Only £160,000 of the £180,000 earned in Year 3 is required to complete the payback.

Assuming linearity of cash flow the payback period will be 2.89 years (or approximately 2 years and 11 months to the nearest whole month).

The corresponding period for Option B is 3.125 years (3 years and 2 months).

(2 marks for each correct payback period)

TIP

A common error is for candidates to mistake the year in which payback occurs with the number of years it takes, e.g. payback for Option A occurs 11 months into Year 3 – therefore in 2 years and 11 months.

NPV:

Year	Option A Net cash flow (£000s)	Discount Factor	£000s	Option B Net cash flow (£000s)		£000s
0	−400	1.00	−400	−950	1.00	−950
1	+100	0.91	91	+250	0.91	227.5
2	+140	0.83	116.2	+300	0.83	249
3	+180	0.75	135	+350	0.75	262.5
4	+210	0.68	142.8	+400	0.68	272
5	+230	0.62	142.6	+450	0.62	279
		Total	+227.6			+340

The NPV for Option A is £227,600, and £340,000 for Option B. Option B should be chosen on purely financial grounds.

(2 marks for each correct NPV and 1 mark for statement of best option)   **9 marks**

(iii) The limitations of investment appraisal technique are:

■ payback gives no idea of the overall project profitability
■ the results are only as good as the initial data on cash flow. These are highly subjective when projected several years ahead
■ the opportunity cost of capital can change over the life of the project
■ the ARR method ignores the time value of money

(1 mark for each point plus 1 mark for development of a point)   **3 marks**

(b) Economic factors to be considered should include:
■ The state of the economy. The advent of a recession would hit spending on luxury items. Conversely, the return of the 'feel good' factor among consumers will boost sales.
■ Likely tax changes. Is the government about to impose extra direct taxes on the high earners who make up most of Gregory's market?
■ Movement in interest rates. Gregory's is contemplating spending between £½m and £1m on expansion. Most of this finance is likely to be borrowed, therefore any interest rate changes will have a direct impact on the projected cash flows. Increases in interest rates will also reduce the disposable income of the customers.

Market factors to be considered should include:

■ The price and income elasticities of demand for the fashion market. This will indicate how responsive the market is to changes in price and income. Gregory's sales will be more volatile where the elasticities are higher.
■ The degree of competition in the luxury fashion market and the likelihood of new entrants.
■ The likely growth in demand in the current area compared to the growth expected in the nearby town. Option B may be a better option if the existing market is approaching saturation.

(1 + 1 for each point and development. NB The comments must be case-related, mentioning Gregory's by name and the luxury fashion market)   **10 marks**

6. (a) (i) Moving Average of Q1, Q2, Q3, Q4 of 1997 = (110 + 125 + 160 + 130)/4
                                                        = 525/4 = 131.25

Moving Average of Q2, Q3, Q4 of 1997 and Q1 of 1998 = (125 + 160 + 130 + 120)/4
                                                        = 535/4 = 133.75

Trend Q3, 1997 = (131.25 + 133.75)/2 = 132.5

The seasonal variation = Actual sales − trend = 160 − 132.5 = 27.5   **4 marks**

(ii)

	Q1	Q2	Q3	Q4
1995			10.62	−0.63
1996	−8.75	−7.5	20.62	−1.88
1997	−16.25	−5.00	27.5	
Total	−25.00	−12.5	58.74	−2.51
Average seasonal variation	−12.5	−6.25	19.58	−1.26

2 marks

(iii)

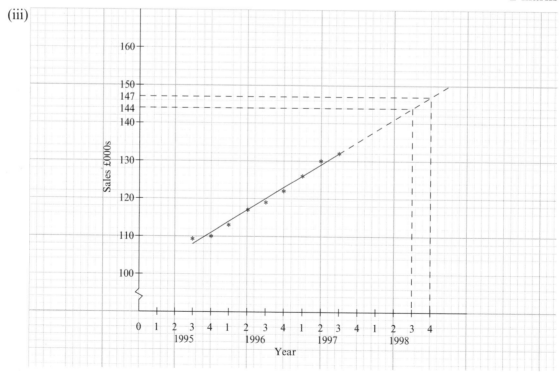

Extending the line of best fit beyond Q3 1997 gives estimates of the trend for Q3 and Q4 1998 of £144,000 and £147,000 respectively. These must be adjusted for seasonal factors.

Estimate for Q3 1998 = Estimated trend + average seasonal variation
$$= £144,000 + £19,380$$
$$= £163,380$$

Estimate for Q4 1998 = Estimated trend + average seasonal variation
$$= £147,000 - £1,260$$
$$= £145,740$$

(2 marks each for a correct estimate of the trend to within $+/-£2000$ plus 1 mark each for seasonal adjustment) **6 marks**

> **TIP**
>
> A forecast requires a two-step approach. First estimate the trend and then adjust for the average seasonal variation. The latter stage is often neglected under exam time pressure.

    (iv)   The shortcomings of time-series forecasting include:

- the assumption that past performance is a good guide to the future
- changes in technology can make past sales data irrelevant, e.g. the sales of typewriters at the launch of the word processor
- new competitors may distort the existing market and seriously affect market share
- it is assumed that seasonality can be 'averaged', e.g. sales of gas and electricity in mild and severe winters
- projections beyond 6 months are highly sceptical

(1 + 1 mark for each point and development or example) **3 marks**

(b)   (i)   **Advantages** of using wholesalers include:

- reduces distribution transport costs as the manufacturer can deliver in bulk
- wholesaler promotes the goods for Zulu Enterprises
- they have well-established links with retailers
- wholesalers bear the cost of storage
- provide a source of market research by feeding back information from retailers

Disadvantages of using wholesalers include:

- profit margin is reduced
- may not promote goods rigorously enough or target the right type of market
- increases the price to the end customer

(1 mark for each of two advantages and two disadvantages) **4 marks**

   (ii)   **Marketing** implications of dealing direct with retailers include:

- Zulu Enterprises can target retailers that fit with its products' image
- need for a sales force adequately trained in the products available from Zulu Enterprises
- increase in direct marketing literature
- opportunity for better market feedback

Financial implications of dealing direct with retailers include:

- cost of setting up a distribution network, e.g. extra transport
- cost of sales force
- cost of increased advertising
- better profit margin

(points must refer to the specific case study: 1 + 1 marks for each point and development) **6 marks**

Solutions to Paper 1, Part 2

Objectives and the business environment

1. Direct taxes are primarily taxes on income (they can also be taxes on capital). Top rates for income tax in the UK have been as high as 83% but have been reduced significantly since 1979. The standard rate of income tax has also been reduced and there is a relatively new lower rate of tax. Behind all these changes is the belief that high direct taxes act as a disincentive to effort and that an employee is more likely to work hard when he sees the reward (income) for his efforts. Paradoxically, the employee will probably pay the same amount in total tax with a reduction in direct taxes being balanced by an increase in indirect taxes! **3 marks**

2. There are several definitions you could use. The Bolton Report (1971) suggested three key characteristics. They are:

    ■ a small share of its market
    ■ owners who work in and take a personal interest in the business
    ■ not part of another (larger) organisation.

    An alternative legal definition is where, over a period of two years:

    ■ turnover is less than £2,800,000
    ■ assets are equal to or less than £1,400,000
    ■ average number of employees is 50 or less.

TIP

> These financial figures may be revised to take account of inflation – you should check with your tutor for up-to-date figures.

Small firms are said to exist for a variety of reasons, including:

■ they perform tasks for which large firms are ill-suited, e.g. servicing niche markets
■ they are often more efficient than large firms, e.g. lower overhead costs
■ they can adjust more rapidly to changed market conditions than large firms
■ they are the vehicle for exploiting the innovations of individuals
■ they are the traditional 'breeding ground' for new industries **5 marks**

3. Changes in the structure of the population provide opportunities for and threats to the business community. For example, a declining birth rate has negative implications for all those involved in providing goods and services for this sector, whilst a growth in the number of pensioners provides opportunities to exploit. The aim of any business organisation should be to monitor its environment so as to identify and respond to these threats and opportunities in good time. **4 marks**

4. The reason why an organisation can charge different prices is because it can identify different segments of its market, each of which has a different elasticity of demand. This means that maximum total revenue for each segment of the market will be achieved at different prices. These segments must be capable of being separated.

    As an example let us consider the case of a rail company. This particular market can be segmented into young people, pensioners, families, students, and business travellers. Let us consider the situations of just two – businessmen and pensioners on a journey to London. The businessman probably has a meeting to get to. He needs to work whilst travelling. He has to travel on a specific train. There are few other forms of travel he could consider. His firm will pay his expenses. We could define him as cash-rich but time-poor. The demand curve for this segment of the market could therefore be described as relatively inelastic. The businessman will be prepared to pay a high price to get what he wants. On the other hand, the pensioner has to pay his own fare and has plenty of time. He would also consider other forms of travel which are cheaper but slower. This segment could be described as time-rich but cash-poor. In this segment of the market the demand curve is far more elastic and the train company would charge a far lower price to achieve maximum total revenue.

There are several other examples you could give, such as airlines, travel agents and phone companies. More recently, a major supermarket has also been experimenting its market along the lines of the example given above by giving discounts to those people that are able to shop at less popular times of the day! **5 marks**

5. Clear and unambiguous objectives are needed so that the organisation may:

   ■ plan for the future
   ■ devise an organisation structure that is effective with all parts contributing to objectives
   ■ motivate employees by providing them with targets to achieve
   ■ direct employees' efforts more effectively
   ■ check how far the goals of the organisation have been achieved and what, if any, corrections are necessary. **3 marks**

Marketing

1. As there is no yardstick by which to judge what should be the price of an entirely new product two approaches have evolved. **Penetration pricing** involves setting a low price to reach as large a market as quickly as possible. It would be used where the firm believes the product may be price sensitive or where it is wished to discourage early competition from other organisations. The major problem with this particular strategy is that if the product's life cycle is short there may be insufficient time to recoup development costs. **Skim pricing** is an alternative strategy which enables development costs to be recovered quickly. A high price is charged on entry to the market. Prices will be lowered as competition emerges and/or sales increase. For skim pricing to work, though, there must be buyers willing to pay a premium price, and the product must be patented so as to prevent early competition. **5 marks**

2. The main functions of packaging are:

   ■ to protect the product in storage and distribution from breakage or deterioration
   ■ to protect employees and customers when handling the product
   ■ to reduce insurance and storage costs
   ■ to gain the interest of the consumer
   ■ to reinforce the messages of branding and promotion. **4 marks**

3. A forecast is a prediction of what is likely to happen in the future. It is most commonly based on past experience. The aim is to reduce future uncertainty and to plan the implications of the changes for the firm. If the demand for the product is likely to rise, this has implications for all the functional departments. For example, production might need to consider different methods of production or another production line. The finance department has to consider how much more working capital will be needed and how to raise this extra finance. The personnel department will have to reconsider its manpower plan in the light of decisions taken by the production and other departments. Marketing will need to reconsider its promotional strategy and perhaps try to identify segments of the market where modified product offerings will be popular. **4 marks**

> **TIP**
>
> In any question where you are asked to explain why a firm does something or the impact of certain actions on the firm, you should always consider the implications for each of the major functional departments.

4. Industrial goods are items where the user is a manufacturer or the provider of a service. Examples could include raw materials, manufactured parts, fixed assets or office equipment. Commercial goods are those where the end user is a consumer, for example food, personal clothing, toiletries. **2 marks**

> **TIP**
>
> Make sure your examples do not have a use in both sectors. Giving the example of a computer as an industrial good is not particularly clever because it has so many uses in the home today (and vice versa).

5. In many industries there are seasonal and cyclical fluctuations in the demand for a product. These fluctuations often make it difficult to predict the general trend. Hotel and catering is a good example of an industry with this problem. A moving average is a quick and easy way of smoothing out these variations in data in order to reveal the underlying trend.   **3 marks**

6. An extension strategy is an attempt to extend the maturity phase of a particular product's life cycle. Extension strategies include finding new markets or new uses for the product, changing the physical appearance of the product or packaging to appeal to new tastes or changing technical specifications. Examples could include the marketing of Lucozade as a 'health' drink or Johnson's baby products as suitable for those with delicate skins!   **2 marks**

Accounting and finance

1. Profit is important to a business because:

   ■ it is the means by which investors judge the success of their investment
   ■ healthy profits mean that the firm is able to raise more money from investors for future plans
   ■ it provides funds for future investments
   ■ it provides reserves which may be drawn upon in difficult times
   ■ it provides a guide to resource allocation between different projects   **6 marks**

2. The payback method of assessing investment projects identifies how long it is before the project pays for itself. It does not take account of the profitability of the project. This method is popular where:

   ■ a firm has only limited resources available and wants to re-invest those funds as soon as possible
   ■ the business environment is unpredictable. Using this method reduces the risk to the firm.   **4 marks**

3. The published financial accounts provide the information necessary for investors to judge the success of their investment, but they also provide information which may be useful to competitors. The dilemma for the firm is to satisfy the shareholders' need for information without revealing too much of the firm's current strategy and future plans.   **3 marks**

4. Fixed costs are those costs which do not vary with the level of business activity. For example, the rent and rates have to be paid whatever the level of operations.

   Variable costs are costs which change with the level of the firm's activity. Thus if output is increased by 25% we would expect labour and power to increase by the same amount.   **3 marks**

5. The formula for calculating the Return on Capital Employed is:

   $$\frac{\text{Profit before interest and taxation}}{\text{Capital Employed}} \times 100$$ **2 marks**

6. Many fixed assets such as vehicles and machines have only a limited lifespan. Throughout their life the value is falling dependent upon the use made of them in any financial period. Depreciation is the charge made to the profit and loss account to reflect their use in that financial period. Without this charge profits would be overstated as would the value of the asset in the balance sheet.   **2 marks**

Human resources

1. Certain activities are essential if an organisation is going to survive. The departments that undertake these activities are termed 'line departments'. As organisations grow, though, line managers find more and more of their time is taken up with other activities, e.g. personnel issues. When the organisation creates a separate Personnel department it has created a staff department. This department has a supportive function and helps improve the efficiency of line activities.

4 marks

2. The span of control is the number of people for whom a manager has direct control. It has been suggested that a manager cannot efficiently control the work of more than 6 subordinates where their work interlocks. Management style is affected by the span of control insofar as a wide span of control is incompatible with democratic or consultative styles of management. The wider the span of control the greater the likelihood of an autocratic style of management and managing through rules and regulations.

4 marks

3. There are numerous constraints on trade union power, including:
   - demand for the finished product
   - market demand for labour
   - attitude of the government
   - attitude of the members
   - impact of new technology
   - labour cost as a proportion of total cost

3 marks

4. Job enrichment is the process of widening the scope of the job to give workers more responsibility, for example allowing them to decide how to carry out their work.

   It is argued that this greater responsibility has a motivating effect upon the employee. In terms of Maslow's theory of motivation it allows the employee to achieve the higher-level needs. In terms of Herzberg's theory the greater responsibility is a 'satisfier'.

3 marks

5. Barriers to communication in a hierarchical organisation could include:
   - overlong transmission mechanism
   - time delay
   - differing status of parties
   - misinterpretation/selection of material
   - feedback may not be received

6 marks

TIP

Remember to answer the question set! There are many barriers to communication in an organisation; not all of them relate to the hierarchical structure of the organisation.

Operations management

1. The advantages of batch production over job production include:
   - a larger output can be produced
   - less skilled labour can be employed
   - compared to job production it may lead to a saving in the amount of machinery used
   - unit cost likely to be lower as fixed costs can be spread over more units of production
   - it provides opportunities for quality control as the batch moves through each process
   - it provides opportunities for developing a costing system, allocating costs to each area and therefore to each product

4 marks

2. The objectives of stock management are:
   - to control all purchases made by the organisation from time of receipt until their issue to production

- to maintain acceptable levels of stocks and ensure that production is not hindered by 'stockouts'.
- to purchase requirements for the operation at the time of need and not before i.e. as in EPOS/JIT Management
- to ensure good stock rotation
- to control 'shrinkage' within the organisation **4 marks**

3. The formula for the Economic Order Quantity is:

$$EOQ = \frac{2CD}{H}$$

where

C = cost of placing an order
D = annual rate of demand
H = cost of holding one unit of stock for a year **2 marks**

 TIP

As in the above question, make sure you define any symbols used.

4. CAD/CAM is the use of a computer in the design and manufacturing of a product. Computer Aided Design (CAD) enables three-dimensional models to be created and rotated on a computer screen. It is possible to change product specifications to test for stress or to optimise on the use of materials. **(1)**

Computer Aided Manufacturing (CAM) refers to the use of computers in controlling the production process. **(1)** Examples of CAM include:

- robots or computer controlled arms that can perform tasks such as welding or bolting parts together
- computer numerically controlled (CNC) machine tools which can be programmed to punch holes, cut shapes or grind materials down
- automatic guided vehicles for materials movement within an operations area. **4 marks**

5. The aim of lean manufacturing is 'continuously to eliminate waste and delay at every stage from raw material to final customer and from concept to market'.

   (a) For suppliers lean manufacturing tends to lead to long-term partnerships with the manufacturing organisation resulting in quality-assured components (which can be delivered direct to the production line), just-in-time delivery (smaller quantities, more frequently) and lower prices (based on better design). **3 marks**
   (b) For employees it tends to lead to working in teams, working flexibly, being responsible for sceduling of work, output and quality levels. Employees would also be expected to take part in the 'continuous improvement of the production process'. **3 marks**

Solutions to Paper 1, Part 3 (Case study)

Section A
1. Briefly explain the following terms as used in the text:
   (a) Limited company
   It is a business unit which is established and regulated by the various Companies Acts. One key feature of such a business unit is that if the business fails, people who have invested money in the firm cannot lose any of their personal possessions – their liability is limited to what they have put into the firm. Limited liability gives the small investor more confidence to invest in companies. **2 marks**

(b) Venture capitalist

Venture capital companies provide capital when funds are not readily available from traditional sources such as banks or the stock market. Funds in excess of £100,000 are lent to small or medium-sized firms in return for an equity stake in the business. Many of these companies are subsidiaries of other financial institutions such as banks, pension funds or insurance companies. **2 marks**

(c) Price elasticity of demand

The sensitivity of quantity demanded to changes in price is known as the price elasticity of demand. It is calculated as follows:

$$\frac{\text{Percentage change in quantity demanded}}{\text{Percentage change in price}}$$

A price elasticity of 3 indicates that the firm faces a very elastic demand curve with a small percentage reduction in price resulting in a more than proportionate increase in the quantity demanded. **2 marks**

(d) Productivity

This is a measure of the efficiency of production. It shows the relationship between factor inputs (the most commonly used measure is labour) and output. An increase in productivity occurs when output per employee is raised. As in the case study, this is most commonly achieved by making better use of or increasing the amount of capital. **2 marks**

(e) Core objective

A core objective is one that identifies the fundamental purpose of an organisation. As in the case study they are often very general in nature. They are also intended to be relatively permanent. Redefining your core objectives implies that major changes are going to be made in products/services made and the markets served. **2 marks**

2. (a) Calculate for Morrow Brothers Ltd:

(i) the contribution per unit

The selling price of the packs is £10.00. The variable costs are labour – £2.50 and materials – £5.50. A total of £8.00. The contribution is therefore £2.00 (£10.00 – £8.00). **2 marks**

(ii) the break-even output

This is calculated by dividing fixed costs by the contribution per unit. Fixed costs are £800,000 and the contribution is £2.00

$$\frac{\text{Fixed costs}}{\text{Contribution}} = \frac{800,000}{2} = 400,000 \text{ units}$$ **2 marks**

> **TIP**
>
> Make sure you show your formulae and calculations.

(iii) the margin of safety

The margin of safety is the amount by which the selected operating point exceeds the break-even point. MBL has sales of £5 million a year. At £10 per unit sale price this is 500,000 units a year. The break-even point was 400,000 units, so the margin of safety must be 100,000 units (i.e. 500,000 – 400,000). **2 marks**

(b) Based on the findings of the consultant (line 53), what would be the new margin of safety?

The break-even point has changed because fixed costs have increased to 900,000. The contribution per unit remains at £2, so the new break-even point is 450,000 units.

The consultant estimated that sales could fall by 10% from £5 million to £4.5 million. This is the equivalent of 450,000 units. Therefore there is no margin of safety, the firm is just breaking even. **4 marks**

3. **The future success of the firm may depend on the decisions the owners of MBL are about to take. Analyse and evaluate the factors you think should be considered before the decision is taken to sell direct to retailers.** **15 marks**

   LEVEL 1   Candidate shows superficial understanding of the issues with only 1 or 2 relevant points.   **(1–3 marks)**

   LEVEL 2   Candidate attempts analysis of the factors affecting the decision but the answer lacks clarity.   **(4–7 marks)**

   LEVEL 3   Candidate analyses factors in depth.   **(8–11 marks)**

   LEVEL 4   Evaluation based on own analysis.   **(12–15 marks)**

Points to make include:

- The brothers are right to be concerned. Based on the industry average of £2,500 profit per employee, the firm should be making profits in the region of £375,000.

- The information given suggests that this is very much a production-orientated firm with little marketing expertise. By implication and with no other information we can say that it is the marketing function that is the cause of the problem,

- Changing distribution channel is a major decision. It is difficult, takes a long time and is costly. The lack of marketing expertise suggests that for MBL it could be very difficult.

- The financial implications of change are also significant. We have already seen that on the consultants figures the firm will just break-even in the first year. It would be advisable for the brothers to assume that they could even move into a loss-making situation. In which case, have they the reserves to sustain a period of losses? If not, are they able to raise the money? Certainly the firm is profitable at present but it doesn't seem to be doing as well as it should (refer to the lower than expected profits for MBL's size).

- From the case study we note that competition in the industry is intense with many firms working on wafer-thin profit margins. The firm is also selling an undifferentiated product where price is likely to remain the critical factor. Whatever distribution channel is used the degree of competi-tion is going to be high.

- The brothers also have to consider their reaction to the possibility of purchasing Wilson's Ltd. If they believe that this is a reasonable proposition then they have to consider whether they have the resources, time and money, to take both this and the change in distribution channel forward at the same time.

TIP

> In any case study you will find that there are two or three really key factos which emerge. Concentrating on analysing the implications of these factors will bring you most of the marks.

The Wilson proposal is interesting because the firm is operating in a slightly different part of the market. It is obvious that the firm is not doing particularly well at the moment but as recently as 1994 it had a return on capital employed of nearly 36% (6% profit margin × 5.9 net asset turnover ratio. It would seem it has been far easier to earn a good return in this market.

The venture capitalist company should also be consulted as they own 35% of the shares. Many venture capitalists are prepared to give advice to the firms they invest in. Often they have functional experts (e.g. marketing) who can go into an organisation to investigate a problem.

4. (a)   **What do you understand by the term 'paternalistic management style' (line 10)**
   A paternalistic manager is very like an autocratic manager in that he sets the objectives, makes the decisions and insists on compliance with those decisions. This style is adopted on the basis 'I know best'. A manager who has a paternalistic style of management is unlikely to be such a hard taskmaster as an autocrat. He would also have a greater interest in his subordinates as individuals. The style leads to subordinates being very dependent on their manager and a crisis of succession. The style may also lead to dissatisfaction amongst employees.   **5 marks**

(b) **Assess the logic of Morrow Brothers Ltd's policy of appointing staff on the basis of recommendation of existing employees.** **10 marks**

> **LEVEL 1** Candidate shows only superficial understanding of the issues with only 1 or 2 relevant points. **(1–3 marks)**
>
> **LEVEL 2** Candidate develops 3 or more relevant points. **(4–7 marks)**
>
> **LEVEL 3** Candidate assesses logic of appointing staff on the basis of recommendation. **(8–10 marks)**

Points to make include:

- may have some logic if the brothers want the organisation to function like one big happy family
- saves time and money
- it is more likely that the person will 'fit in' because they are already known to at least some members of the firm and probably know something about the firm themselves.
- has potential for creating a strong informal organisation. This may be of benefit to or cause problems for the firm
- doesn't guarantee that the firm is getting the best person for the job in terms of skills and work experience
- there could be problems if people 'fall out' socially with the dispute being continued at work
- there could be clashes at work with different employees each wanting to promote their own candidate for a vacancy

5. **To what extent do you believe that it would have been possible for MBL to have avoided unrest amongst the employees during the recent period of change?** **10 marks**

> **LEVEL 1** Candidate shows only superficial understanding of the issues with only 1 or 2 relevant points. **(1–3 marks)**
>
> **LEVEL 2** Candidate develops 3 or more relevant points. **(4–7 marks)**
>
> **LEVEL 3** Candidate assesses the extent to which MBL could have avoided unrest amongst employees. **(8–10 marks)**

Points to make could include:

- People resist change because of its impact upon them personally. Examples of why people resist change include possibility of redundancy or transfer to another job, reductions in status or pay, the breaking up of social groups or the dislocation of personal life by new working arrangements.
- It would be very unusual for change to take place in any organisation without some unrest and resistance to change on the part of employees, simply because change will always have *some* impact on them.
- The information available suggests that the brothers have actively tried to reduce the level of unrest by giving guarantees of no job losses and the promises of retraining where necessary. Nevertheless, the unrest might be further minimised where:
    1. the need for change is made clear and people are warned of how it is going to affect them, when and why;
    2. involve people in the planning and implementation of change – this makes it more acceptable to them;
    3. social groups are not broken up;
    4. changes are introduced slowly so people can adapt.

TIP
Look at the 'level of response' marking scheme. To obtain a high mark here you are required to make a judgement as to how far the problems could have been avoided.

6. (a)   **On the basis of the information given in Appendix 1, assess the financial position of Wilson's Ltd from 1993 to 1998.**   **15 marks**

 LEVEL 1   Candidate offers superficial view of accounts, with only 1 or 2 valid ratios calculated/used.   **(1–4 marks)**

 LEVEL 2   Candidate uses valid ratios to analyse profit, liquidity and efficiency.
                                                                                                (5–10 marks)

 LEVEL 3   Candidate critically evaluates performance of MBL on the basis of the evidence provided.   **(11–15 marks)**

Content:
Students should make use of the last 5 years' ratios when answering this question.

> **TIP**
>
> You should also be aware that it is possible to calculate the Return on Capital Employed by multiplying the profit margin by the net asset ratio.

Thus, the ratios available for analysis are:

	1993	1994	1995	1996	1997	1998
Return on capital employed	49.6	35.4	16.4	11.7	3.8	3.8
Profit margin	8	6	4	3	2	2
Net asset turnover	6.2	5.9	4.1	3.9	1.9	1.9
Debtors turnover	8.3	9.6	11.4	11.5	11.8	31.0
Stock turnover	7.1	7.3	8.4	9.1	10.0	10.0
Current ratio	2.1	1.9	1.8	1.4	0.98	0.97
Acid test	1.3	1.1	1.0	1.1	0.46	0.46

The ratios present a picture of near-disastrous decline in the performance of this company.

The key ratio – the ROCE – shows a decline from an unusually high 49.6 to a mere 3.8. The reason for this is twofold. First, the profit margin has fallen from an above-industry-average of 8% to 2% (the effects of competition?) and, second, net asset turnover has declined from 8 to 2. In an industry like printing with a low profit margin one would expect to see a higher asset turnover ratio.

The liquidity ratios – current and acid test – reveal a similar picture. In 1993 both ratios were near the acceptable minimum 2:1 and 1:1 respectively. In 1998, with the current ratio at 0.97:1 and the acid test ratio at 0.46:1 the firm is technically insolvent, being unable to pay its debts as and when they become due.

The efficiency ratios – stock and debtor turnover – reveal different stories. The stock turnover ratio has improved over a period when every other ratio is worsening. A rise in the ratio is normally associated with cutting prices to increase turnover or improved marketing effort, but could also be due to a policy of reducing the levels of stock held. In conjunction with the reduction in profit margin the improvement in this ratio might suggest a policy of cutting prices. The number of days taken to collect debts has increased dramatically over the period and suggests there is a problem with the firm's credit control system.

Looking at the ratios for 1998 in comparison with 1997 it would seem that the position has largely stabilised with one important exception – the debtor turnover ratio. The rapid increase here suggests that many of the sales on credit during the last year have been made without consideration being given to the creditworthiness of the customer. Many of these debts may in actual fact be 'bad'.

> **TIP**
>
> Many candidates can calculate these ratios but find difficulty in explaining their results. You should practise this skill with examples from a number of old examination papers.

(b) **Comment on the limitations of your conclusions.** **5 marks**

Comments to make include:

- accounting conventions and the ways certain values are arrived at may have changed, e.g. the basis on which depreciation is calculated
- ratios based on accounts are always out of date – particularly if based on published information
- if comparisons are made over time, inflation may distort the ratios as may changes in exchange rates, interest rates or government policy
- where comparisons are made between firms or across an industrial sector, differences in product mix may render conclusions doubtful
- other non-quantitative information may paint a different picture, e.g. labour relations, customer goodwill, brand image, new product development programme, etc.

Section B

1. **Many people have voiced concern at Directors in a company giving themselves large increases in pay whilst imposing severe pay restraints on their employees.**

Discuss why a firm might pursue such policies. **20 marks**

LEVEL 1 Superficial attempt to answer the question based on common sense. **(1–4 marks)**

LEVEL 2 One-sided argument with a little analysis or a balanced argument with superficial analysis. **(5–8 marks)**

LEVEL 3 One-sided argument but with some good analysis or a balanced answer with some analysis. **(9–12 marks)**

LEVEL 4 Good analysis with some evaluation. **(13–16 marks)**

LEVEL 5 Evaluation of the issues. **(17–20 marks)**

Points to make could include:

- Supply and demand analysis tells us that disproportionately high salaries will have to be paid to retain the services of those with very scarce skills, whilst others with lower-level skills will receive little in the way of increase in wages.
- Weak trade unions cannot protect the interests of their members. This weakness could be the result of legislation, recession, lack of membership, or high unemployment of members with that skill.
- Forced to by other firms who follow this policy (especially true if American links or influences).
- Without legislation or clear principles to guide those in positions of power it is difficult to expect any other kind of behaviour.
- Divorce between ownership and control. Lack of control on the part of shareholders enables Directors to act in their own interests but against those of the owners.
- Financial incentives for those at the top may have a disproportionately bigger effect than incentives for other employees.

2. (a) **With the aid of examples explain, what you understand by the term 'social responsibility' and why it is desirable.** **8 marks**

An organisation is not only affected by its environment; it can, in turn, affect that environment. For example a firm may pollute the atmosphere or the river. It can make some of its employees redundant. By bribery it may obtain business which would otherwise have gone elsewhere. An organisation is deemed to be socially responsible when it is concerned with the impact of its actions on the physical, social, economic or political environment. This is sometimes termed the *stakeholder approach* to social responsibility.

A much more limited view of social responsibility is put forward in the *shareholder approach* which argues that the firm's responsibility is limited to its owners and to their interests (profit and long-term growth of the business). The firm is not concerned with any other issues. These are the responsibility of government.

In its broader sense, social responsibility is desirable because otherwise a firm may use its power to appropriate an unfair share of social benefits, forcing other firms or society as a whole to bear these costs.

(b) **How effective are the ways in which society can encourage firms to become more socially responsible?** **(12 marks)**

LEVEL 1 Candidate has identified 1 or more relevant points. **(1–3 marks)**

LEVEL 2 Candidate has demonstrated an understanding of the issues involved. **(4–8 marks)**

LEVEL 3 Candidate has displayed evaluation through examining the issues and and making valid judgements and conclusions. **(9–12 marks)**

Points to make include:

■ Change the culture of the company. In practice this is difficult because almost inevitably the stock exchange and shareholders assess the company on the basis of its financial results. Equally, individual managers are assessed by how well they control costs, not how socially responsible they are. However, where a firm is acting irresponsibly, encourage whistle-blowing by employees in the know (but is the employee willing to risk losing his or her job?).

■ Self-regulatory codes of conduct. A situation where the industry establishes rules of conduct for all its members. This is policed by the industry and fines may be levied where there are breaches. Cynics would argue that codes of conduct are a smokescreen to avoid legislation and that by and large they are ineffective, e.g. the press and its code of conduct regarding invasion of privacy. Both government and industry like this idea because costs of regulation through legislation are so high.

■ Market mechanisms. Encourage consumers to purchase from socially responsible firms (though there are difficulties here because what may be socially responsible to one person may not be to another, e.g. is it better to accept a polluted atmosphere or close the factory down?). The Blue Angel, the German eco-friendly label, covers some 4,000 products and is recognised by 80% of the German population. Some shops, e.g. The Body Shop base their market appeal on environmental grounds. Nevertheless, there is a lot of evidence to show that many consumers are very price conscious and unwilling to pay extra.

■ In the UK there is evidence that banks are more careful now in lending to firms where there is the risk of environmental damage (and for which that firm may be made liable). Equally, insurance companies are putting up premiums in line with claims made for environmental damage.

■ External pressure. Can influence the firm by encouraging consumers to boycott products, obtaining media attention, obtaining membership of decision-making bodies, lobbying Parliamant and government and finally by strikes and demonstrations. Their effectiveness depends on public interest, membership and financial resources. In some cases pressure-group interest is effective because the costs of defending themselves against PG pressure are greater than the costs of compliance! Nevertheless, there are many situations where PG pressure is not successful.

■ Government intervention. Direct intervention through the ownership of industry has not proved the industry (government) to be very responsible, e.g. coal mining. Legislation has been more effective but government finds difficulty in financing the system of regulation (e.g. Health and Safety at Work) properly. Another major problem is that this approach tends to make firms adhere to the letter of the law, not the spirit. Legislation may also make firms consider alternative locations for production.

Solutions to Paper 2, Part I

1. (a) Any two ratios from:

- ROCE – this indicates the percentage return that can be generated on the long-term capital employed in the business. It can be compared to other investment opportunities and to other firms in the industry.
- Profit margin – this indicates the amount of profit generated from sales revenue and how vulnerable the business is to any cost increases.
- Gearing – this measures the proportion of capital employed that is provided by long-term lending. A high proportion would indicate that the business profits would suffer if interest rates increased. **4 marks**

(b) **Profitability**

Ratio	1997	1998
ROCE = Operating profit / Total capital employed	= 3240/11 457 * 100 = 28.3%	= 4612/16 265 * 100 = 28.4%
Gross profit margin = Gross profit/Sales	= 7200/21 600 * 100 = 33.3%	= 8007/25 624 * 100 = 31.2%
Net profit margin = Net profit/Sales	= 3240/21 600 * 100 = 15%	= 4612/25 624 * 100 = 18%
Asset utilisation ratio = Sales/Capital employed	= 21 600/11 457 = 1.89	= 25 624/16 265 = 1.58

Overall profitability at B.J. Amin has remained steady at just over 28%. Although the gross profit has fallen by 1.1%, the net profit has risen 3%, probably due to better control of overheads and indirect expenses. It is noted, however, that the assets are not being worked as hard to generate sales as the AUR has fallen from 1.89 to 1.58.

Financial status:

Ratio	1997	1998
Current ratio = Current assets/current liabilities	= 5761/4522 = 1.27	= 9827/5862 = 1.68
Acid Test = Current assets – stock / current liabilities	= 2543/4522 = 0.56	= 4015/5862 = 0.68
Gearing = Long-term liabilities / Total capital employed	= 5860/11 457 = 0.51	= 2724/16 265 = 0.17

The current ratios indicate that B.J. Amin has sufficient funds to meet short-term debts but the acid test ratios show that there is a need for more working capital. In 1998 too much finance is tied up in stock and debtors. These need to be better managed in order to release finance to meet current liabilities. The gearing is low at 0.17, therefore B.J. Amin could raise liquid funds through borrowing without too much risk from interest rate increases.

(1 mark for each correctly calculated ratio and 1 mark for use of it in commenting on B.J. Amin's profitability or financial status) **10 marks**

(c) The use of ratios as a guide to future performance is limited because:

- gross profits can be affected by increased competition
- net profits can be affected by changes in overhead costs or changes in interest rates
- sales can be affected by new technology or changes in customer preferences
- the general economy can could slow down causing sales to fall and prices squeezed downwards
- changes in management personnel can greatly affect profitability
- exchange rates might change affecting both the cost of imported raw materials, prices of foreign goods and the export price of B.J. Amin's products

(1 mark for any reasonable comment about the uncertainty of predicting performance in a dynamic economy) **3 marks**

(d)   Benefits of introducing new information technology include:

■ better stock management
■ lower risk of stock shortages
■ analysis of product popularity
■ identification of slow movers
■ identification of older stock prior to its sell-by date
■ analysis of individual store requirements which should lead to better profiling of the local customers' needs
■ central bulk ordering and bulk discounts available
■ less need for administrative staff at local level

Costs include:

■ initial cost of computer hardware and software
■ training costs for staff   **8 marks**

Level 3 (7–8 marks)
Answer evaluates the effect on B.J. Amin of new technology mentioning benefits for both better stock management and better marketing data. Balances the cost of the technology against the benefits.

Level 2 (4–6 marks)
Analyses the pros and cons of a computerised system in the context of the case study but might only concentrate on one aspect or one side of the argument.

Level 1 (1–3 marks)
Simply lists a number of advantages or costs without specific reference to the case study.

2. (a)

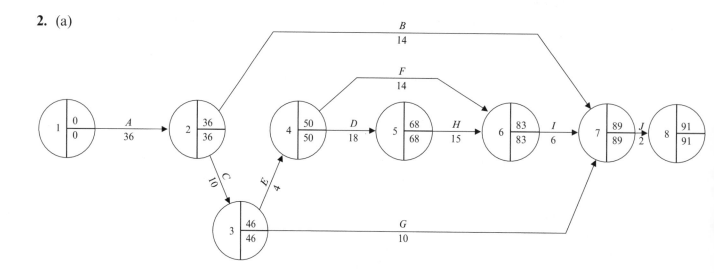

(Deduct 1 mark for each logic error and $\frac{1}{2}$ mark for missing arrow heads)   **7 marks**

(b) From the critical path diagram it can be seen that the critical activities are ACEDHIJ and that the project will take 91 days. This means the extension will not be ready in time for the arrival of the American party.

(2 marks each for correct identification of critical path and project duration. 1 mark for correct comment). **5 marks**

(c) The project can only be reduced by shortening the time taken to complete critical activities **(1)** therefore A, C, and H should be targeted with extra labour **(2)**. This will cost £80 + £70 + £60 = £210 in total **(2)**. **5 marks**

TIP

Reducing one critical activity might make other activity paths to become critical. Always check the effect of changes on the diagram.

(d) Answers might include:

- improved booking arrangements that avoids double-booking of hotel rooms and tracks occupancy levels
- better, accurate and faster customer billing service that avoids long waits at check-out and missed items for payment
- allows building of a client database for market analysis and more accurate targeting of customers with special offers in quiet periods
- improved accounting procedures allowing faster analysis of cost centre information
- cost savings on administrative staff leading to improved profitability **8 marks**

Level 3 (7–8 marks)
Answer evaluates the effect on a hotel of new technology mentioning benefits for two different applications.

Level 2 (4–6 marks)
Analyses the pros and cons of a computerised system in the context of the case study but might only concentrate on the benefits of one application.

Level 1 (1–3 marks)
Simply lists a number of applications and/or benefits of IT without meaningful reference to La Hacienda or a hotel.

3. (a) (i) Break-even output $= \dfrac{\text{Fixed costs}}{\text{Contribution per unit}}$

where fixed costs $= £4.40 * 200,000 = £880,000$

and Contribution $=$ Price $-$ variable costs

$$= £26 - (£9 + £2 + £4) = £11$$

therefore break-even $= £880,000/£11 = 80,000$ chairs

(1 mark for each of correct equation, fixed costs, contribution and correct calculation) **4 marks**

(ii) Margin of safety $=$ Current or proposed output $-$ break-even output **(1)**

$$= 180,000 - 80,000 = 100,000 \text{ units } (1)$$ **2 marks**

TIP

Always state the equation in full and not in shorthand form.

(b) (i) Assuming fixed costs are covered by current output the special order would make the following unit contribution:

Unit Contribution = Price − variable costs

$$= £17 - (£15 + £0.60) = £1.40 \textbf{ (1)}$$

therefore the total contribution of the special order would be

$$(20,000 * £1.40) = £28,000 \textbf{ (1)}$$

This is the same as the special design costs and therefore the order would add nothing to overall profitability **(1)**. On purely numerical grounds there appears to be no reason for accepting the order **(1)**.   **4 marks**

TIP

Whenever the expression 'special order' is mentioned, look to use contribution costing. As long as it is not a negative contribution it might be worth doing depending on non-financial considerations.

(ii) Although the order does not add to immediate profits the firm should take account of the following positive and negative factors before making a final decision:

Positive factors:

■ further orders might be forthcoming from this large customer on which the special design cost will not apply
■ it opens up a new market in Europe
■ it uses up spare capacity
■ it might allow raw materials to be purchased at a greater discount
■ it increases the margin of safety
■ firm can remain in the deluxe market

Negative factors
■ reaction of workforce to full-capacity working
■ new venture postponed which might be more profitable
■ how reliable is the French company at paying promptly?
■ possibility of unfavourable exchange rate changes

(1 + 1 marks for each point and development)   **7 marks**

(c) The available pricing policies include:

■ Cost-plus pricing – adding a profit margin to the full cost of the new chair. This may or may not be sufficient to compete with existing producers in this market segment.
■ Competitive pricing – setting prices at the prevailing prices in the market place. This would require Design Mouldings to compete on non-price factors such as the quality of the product or aggressive marketing.
■ Penetration pricing – setting prices below current market levels in order to build market share. This is a high-risk option as profit margins are low and it might trigger a price war with existing competitors.   **8 marks**

Level 3 (7–8 marks)
Answer evaluates the pricing strategies balancing the pros and cons of each and coming to a reasoned judgement based on the market for budget-priced chairs.

Level 2 (4–6 marks)
Analyses the pros and cons of one or more pricing strategies in the context of the case study.

Level 1 (1–3 marks)
Simply lists a number of pricing methods without meaningful reference to the market for low-priced chairs.

TIP

Ensure that your recommendation about the choice of pricing strategy fits the type of product and market.

4. (a) Any two from:

- customers
- suppliers
- financiers
- the local community
- government   **2 marks**

(b) Points that might be used in the comparison include:

- For the shopfloor worker being paid a low wage:
  - a low-skilled job that many can do with little training
  - supply and demand determines the wage paid
  - comparable wages are paid for similar jobs in other organisations
  - low level of responsibility and decision making
- For the executives being paid a high wage:
  - a payment for exceptional skill
  - short in supply but high in demand
  - high rewards needed to retain successful executives as they are highly mobile and actively sought after
  - high level of responsibility and decision-making that might be crucial to the survival and profitability of the organisation

But candidates might argue that:

- market value is very hard to prove
- many of the executives were willing to work for much lower salaries when the industry was nationalised
- executive pay is set by other executives who have a vested interest in maintaining high rewards for this group of people
- the high rewards and the large spread of wages might be bad for morale within the organisation, producing an 'us and them' relationship.   **8 marks**

Level 3 (7–8 marks)
Answer evaluates the arguments for and against a free market approach to wage settlements, mentioning most of the points outlined above.

Level 2 (4–6 marks)
Analyses the pros and cons of the argument in the context of the case study, mentioning some of the points given above.

Level 1 (1–3 marks)
Candidate shows some understanding of the problem and makes some attempt at comparison of the arguments for and against but may not relate it to the case study.

(c) (i) A financial incentive that offers workers the right to buy shares in the company at a future date at a pre-set price. The hope is that the share price will rise through the efforts of the workforce at improving profitability For example a worker might be given the option of buying 2000 shares at 50p at any time between 2 and 3 years later. If the company performs well and the share price rises to, say, 90p then the worker can exercise their right to buy and either sell immediately and make £800 profit or hold the shares hoping for further gains. It is hoped that this type of remuneration scheme will reinforce loyalty to the company among its workforce.   **4 marks**

(ii) **Positive** attitudes might include:

- a clear link between effort of the workforce, profitability of the company and rewards
- a good incentive to work harder
- creates a 'family' atmosphere
- the reward is tax efficient
- regarded as a bonus on top of their normal wage

Negative attitudes might include:

- an uncertain reward
- executives gain the most
- failure to meet the financial targets will result in little gain from taking up the options which might have a demoralising effect

(1 mark per point, positive or negative) **3 marks**

TIP

Remember to consider arguments from both sides unless specifically requested not to do so, e.g. advantages and disadvantages, employees and employer, etc.

(d) Any of the following reasons might be given:

In favour of government intervention:

- pay policy to ensure a decent minimum and to stop exploitation
- to ensure some equity, particularly with wages and conditions of work
- for health and safety reasons
- to prevent inflation
- to ensure environmental costs are considered

Against government intervention:

- market forces are more effective at directing scarce resources
- it is the shareholders' responsibility as owners of the company to decide on its policies
- pressure groups are more effective at influencing company policy **8 marks**

Level 3 (7–8 marks)
Answer evaluates the arguments for and against government intervention. Arguments given are directed at the issues raised in the case study.

Level 2 (4–6 marks)
Analyses the pros and cons of the argument in the context of the case study mentioning some of the points given above.

Level 1 (1–3 marks)
Candidate gives some general reasons for intervention but fails to relate to the case study.

5. (a) (i) Brand names are a means of distinguishing a product from its rivals through a name that is heavily advertised. In the article, Coca-Cola, Pepsi and Virgin are all examples of brand names. Successful branding adds value to a product and creates brand loyalty. **2 marks**

(ii) An immature market is one in which there is still scope for expansion for both existing producers and new entrants. In this case Coca-Cola believes the UK has potential for growth as consumers drink only half as much fizzy soft drinks as the American market. **2 marks**

(iii) An own brand or own label is a product bearing the retailer's name that is made by a manufacturer to the retailer's specifications and sold at a price level below that of the brand leader. In the soft drinks market Sainsbury's Classic Cola is an example of a cheaper own brand. **2 marks**

(b) (i) Annual value of Coca-Cola/Pepsi = 78% of £6 billion = £4.68bn **1 mark**

(ii) Annual value of Virgin Cola = 4% of £6 billion = £0.24bn **1 mark**

TIP

Remember that the question asked you to refer to the article and the examiner will expect examples related to the soft drinks market.

(c) (i) Coke and Pepsi are well-established brands backed by enormous promotional budgets. The only way for Virgin to compete is on price and, to a limited extent, on place.

With a lower price Virgin is trying to tempt low-budget consumers to buy its product. Virgin is cleverly using the idea of avoiding a 'brand tax' to persuade consumers to buy a similar quality cola at a lower price.

Virgin's 'place' strategy is based on selling through a major supermarket, Tesco, in order to limit the cost of distribution. Virgin realises that it cannot compete with Coca-Cola's and Pepsi's widespread network without spending a great deal of money. This is not yet possible on their smaller profit margins.

In the long run Virgin will only be a threat if it begins to compete in the small store and vending machine sectors of the market. This will only be a possibility if market share grows and profits improve. **8 marks**

Level 3 (7–8 marks)
Answer evaluates the strategy based on price and place identifying both short-term and long-term objectives.

Level 2 (4–6 marks)
Analyses some of the reasons for the chosen strategy but fails to identify both short- and long-term objectives.

Level 1 (1–3 marks)
Candidate describes the two elements of the chosen strategy but with little explanation of why these approaches have been chosen.

TIP

Strategy involves both short-term and long-term objectives. Many students neglect to assess what the next stage will be and how this relates to the limited view given in the case study.

(ii) Coke and Pepsi are a duopoly as they control over three-quarters of the fizzy drinks market. They already possess well established market leading brands and they are keen to protect their own market share. Competition between the two is fierce. Any loss of market share by one will greatly enhance the profits of the other. They stress promotion, therefore, as a means of maintaining brand loyalty and expanding both existing consumer consumption and capturing new customers. They avoid price competition as this will reduce profit margins without significantly increasing overall sales. They each have a sophisticated and widespread distribution network so place in the UK is not a factor.

(1 + 1 marks for each valid point and development) **5 marks**

(d) Coke and Pepsi do not feel threatened for the following reasons:

■ UK market is still growing
■ consumption is only 150 cans per consumer compared to 300 cans in America
■ own brands and Virgin only compete in the supermarket segment
■ the cost of setting up a wide distribution network is too expensive for its rivals

- large promotion budgets ensure high market share
- as the market expands they will enjoy further economies of scale enabling Coke and Pepsi to increase promotion further or to engage in some limited price reductions

(1 mark for each reasonable point)   **4 marks**

6. (a) **(i)** Decision trees are useful for decision-making where:

- there are clear alternative options
- there is uncertainty that can be measured by probability
- pay-offs for each option can be quantified
- all options are known

(1 mark for each point)   **2 marks**

(ii) Actual values are forecast pay-offs for each course of action. These forecasts might be based on;

- previous outcomes in similar events
- estimates made by market research
- expert opinion
- use of historic data and time series analysis to forecast likely future sales

                                                                                       2 marks

> **TIP**
> All estimates about future outcomes involve uncertainty. It is good practice to remain sceptical about the accuracy of these projections.

(iii) The expected monetary value is the average pay-off if the decision was taken many times. It is found by multiplying the probability of the event occurring by the estimated pay-off for each option available. **(2)**

The unique selling point (USP) is the feature that differentiates a product or business from its competitors. In the case of Suzanne Gregory she feels her knowledgeable staff and reasonably priced goods set her apart from other sports shops in the area. **(2)**

                                                                                       4 marks

(b)

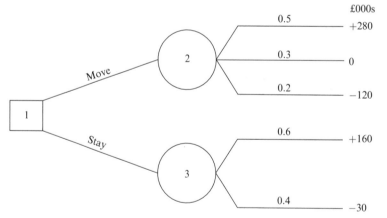

EMV at node No. 2 = (0.5 * +280) + (0.3 * 0) + (0.2 * −120) = +116
EMV at node No. 3 = (0.6 * +160) + (0.4 * −30) = +84

therefore best decision and EMV at node No. 1 is +£116,000.

The optimal decision for Suzanne is to move to the new development as the model, based solely on quantitative data, indicates an increase in net income of £116,000.

(3 marks for a correctly drawn tree, 2 marks for the EMV calculations and 1 mark for the optimum decision)   **6 marks**

> **TIP**
> The decision tree model takes account only of quantitative data. Non-financial factors must also be considered before recommending a final decision.

(c) There are two strategies available:

- attempt to keep existing staff:
  - offer transport, e.g. a shared taxi or mini-bus which would cut down travel time as it would be a direct service
  - increase wages to retain staff for the new site. This might be a temporary measure until new staff could be trained
  - introduce a bonus system linked to the profitability of the new shop. This might act as a large enough incentive to overcome the inconvenience of travel

- train new staff:
  - advertise ahead of the move and train candidates at the existing site
  - wait until the new site is ready and conduct on-the-job training with locally based staff. This might have an effect on sales in the short term but could be a cheaper option than transporting existing staff. **5 marks**

(d) Sources of finance available include:

- Bank loan – Suzanne must be able to convince the bank that her new business proposition is well-researched and viable. She may also have to provide collateral as security for the loan, e.g. her house. This increases the risk of the venture.
- A partnership – if the bank refuse to lend the required sum then Suzanne could look for a partner who would be willing to contribute sufficient finance. The advantage of this is that the capital injected is permanent, but the disadvantage is that profits will have to be shared and Suzanne would lose some of the control over the business.
- Her own savings – if Suzanne has sufficient funds she might consider risking a further capital injection into the business. This is a risky option as she stands to lose it if the new venture fails. On the positive side, if it is successful, she gets to keep all of the profits. **6 marks**

Level 3 (5–6 marks)
Answer evaluates the sources of finance stating the advantages and disadvantages of both options.

Level 2 (3–4 marks)
Describes the sources of finance in the context of the case study but mentions only the advantages or the disadvantages.

Level 1 (1–2 marks)
Candidate describes the sources of finance without reference to the case study.

Solutions to Paper 2, Part 2

Objectives and the business environment

1. The exchange rate means the rate at which we exchange pounds for other currencies. A rise in the exchange rate means that it takes more foreign currency to buy each pound or put the other way round the pound buys more foreign currency. Thus a manufacturer who imports raw materials or components will not have to pay so much for a given quantity of imports. However, when the same manufacturer tries to sell (export) his finished product abroad he will find it more difficult because the importer now has to pay more in the local currency to buy a given amount of pounds. **4 marks**

> **TIP**
> Make sure you cover the situation of a manufacturing firm as an importer **and** an exporter.

2. Because our resources are limited we cannot fulfil all our needs. The purchase of one good implies that we have had to make a sacrifice by not being able to buy something else. This sacrifice that has been made is described by economists as the 'opportunity cost' of buying the other good.

Social costs are those costs which arise out of the use of a product which are not borne by the owner or user of that product. For example the costs of pollution caused by cars are borne by society as a whole rather than the individuals creating that pollution. **4 marks**

3. Oxfam stakeholders would include:

full-time employees, part-time collectors, suppliers of goods, buyers, recipients, funds providers and the local community. **2 marks**

4. The main functions of the business plan include:

■ to offset future uncertainty by producing a future strategy, i.e. objectives, targets and goals
■ to identify resources needed to support the plan
■ to identify the precise way functional units can contribute to the plan
■ to enable the development of an organisational structure appropriate to the plan
■ to act as a means of controlling business operations
■ to ensure that future plans are profitable
■ to provide a means of motivating and appraising individual performance. **6 marks**

5. Economies of scale include:

■ production or technical economies arising from linked processes or longer production runs
■ marketing economies in areas such as purchasing, advertising and selling
■ financial economies such as finding it easier and cheaper to raise capital
■ organisational economies arising from the appointment of specialist staff to relieve line managers of peripheral acivities, e.g. recruitment
■ transportation economies arising from more efficient use of organisations' own vehicles and better rates obtained from outside carriers
■ risk-bearing economies arising from the diversification of business interests and research and development projects. **4 marks**

 TIP

> Try to show the range of your knowledge by giving examples from as many different functional departments as possible.

Marketing

1. Reasons why a firm may sell part of its product line at a loss include:

■ to deter competition from entering a market
■ to penetrate a new market
■ to maintain volume production and avoid laying-off staff
■ in a recession even selling at a 'loss' may result in a contribution being made toward fixed costs
■ products may be sold at a loss because the manufacturer knows that he can make profits on the sale of accessories or related branded goods
■ a retail store may sell certain goods at a loss to attract customers in the hope that they will also purchase other high-profit-margin products. **4 marks**

2. The car market can be segmented in many different ways including quality, economy, size of car, size of family, level of usage, image. **2 marks**

3. Advertising effectiveness may be gauged through changes in the levels of sales and profitability. The effectiveness of a change in advertising revenue could be evaluated by comparing:

$$\frac{\text{Proportionate change in sales volume}}{\text{Proportionate change in promotional expenditure}}$$ **4 marks**

4. The relationship between marketing and production will change in the following ways:

   ■ there may be a higher level of friction as production finds that it has to change its methods and attitudes toward the consumer
   ■ (alternatively) there may be a higher level of co-operation between the two functions
   ■ the marketing department will play a more influential role in product development
   ■ extension strategies will be based on market needs rather than production costs or new technology. **4 marks**

5. The purposes of branding include:

   ■ it is a form of product differentiation helping customers to recognise goods and services and thereby creating a loyalty to the brand
   ■ the more similar the product to competing goods the more necessary it is to distinguish it in the market place
   ■ advertising and promotion need a brand name to sell to customers
   ■ branding leads to greater acceptance of a manufacturers goods by wholesalers and retailers
   ■ it reduces the importance of price differentials between goods and services
   ■ brand loyalty gives an organisation more control over pricing and marketing strategy
   ■ it increases the likelihood of self-selection in supermarkets and other self-service stores
   ■ the brand can be extended to support other products, i.e. the name of one product can be used to sell another product. **4 marks**

6. Sampling may provide innacurate information because:

   ■ there is a bias in the questionnaire
   ■ the data obtained is insufficient to draw conclusions from
   ■ the data may be unrepresentative of normal conditions or be affected by actually being collected (this is sometimes referred to as the 'Hawthorne effect' after Mayo's studies where workers performed better just because they were being studied)
   ■ omission of an important factor
   ■ carelessness in the collection or interpretation of data
   ■ if questions require a complex answer, for example more than one word or sentence, it is sometimes difficult to interpret the results. This is particularly true of 'in-depth' interviews. **4 marks**

Accounting and finance

1. In some situations an organisation may sell goods or provide a service at less than cost, for example where it is operating at less than full capacity. The rationale behind this is that the organisation will reduce losses as long as the price charged is greater than variable costs and thus provides a **contribution** toward fixed costs.

   At its most basic, profit is the difference between revenue and costs. It is possible to distinguish between gross and net profit though with gross profit being the difference between revenue and the cost of goods sold and net profit being the excess of revenue over all expenses. **3 marks**

2. When preparing the profit and loss account, revenue is matched with the costs associated with earning it. This means that revenues and costs are recognised when they are incurred rather than when the cash is received or paid. **3 marks**

3. Sources of finance for a person starting their own business will include savings, remortgage of property, sale of other assets, borrowing from friends, borrowing from a bank and hire purchase. **4 marks**

> **TIP**
>
> There may also be certain sources of government funds available designed to support the firm in its early days.

4. The liquidity ratio is

   $$\frac{\text{Current Assets}}{\text{Current liabilities}}$$

   The ratio is a measure of the ability of the firm to pay its debts as and when they become due. A ratio of less than 2 might suggest that a firm could face difficulties in meeting payments as they become due. **5 marks**

> **TIP**
>
> Note though a ratio of 2 or more could indicate an excessive amount of stock, debtors or cash and an unwillingness to control these items in order to take advantage of profitable opportunities elsewhere.

5. The functions of budgets include:

   ■ to assist in the planning process
   ■ to communicate plans
   ■ to enable co-ordination of departmental acivities
   ■ to motivate staff
   ■ to control and evaluate performance. **2 marks**

Human resources

1. Formal groups are set up by a business to carry out tasks. They are an actual part of the organisation with rules determining their behaviour and actions. In a school a formal group could be the members of a specific department, e.g. history, the senior management team or the administrative/catering support staff. Informal groups are based on individuals with similar interests. They are not part of the formal organisation nor do they have formal rules and regulations to adhere to. However, there are often unofficial norms which influence a member's behaviour. An example of an informal group would be the people who sit and have lunch together in the canteen or employees who sit together in the rest room and talk about last night's snooker on television! **4 marks**

2. Forms of industrial action include strikes, work to rules, go slows, overtime bans, and mass occupation of premises. **3 marks**

3. Actions that the Human Resources Department might take include:

   ■ investigate employment legislation in the overseas market
   ■ investigate salary levels and working conditions in that country
   ■ undertake a skills audit to identify employees with language skills
   ■ revise manpower plan
   ■ advertise for people with the relevant language skills
   ■ develop training programmes to enhance the languge skills of existing employees. **4 marks**

4. The benefits of delegation are:

- it allows the manager to concentrate on more important tasks
- it provides training for the next generation of managers
- it motivates employees by giving them greater responsibilities. **3 marks**

5. (a) In the armed forces the most likely style of leadership is autocratic. By this we mean that the leader is authoritarian and makes decisions without consultation. Communication will be one way with little feedback. Orders are carried out without disagreement or questioning. The autocratic style is seen as being efficient in emergency situations or where there is danger. **3 marks**

    (b) In a research team the most likely style of leadership is democratic. This is an approach where the leader involves the subordinates in the decision-making process with the final decision being made on the basis of consensus. The style is seen as appropriate where team members understand the problem and through their specialist knowledge can contribute in equal measure to the decision. **3 marks**

Operations management

1. Benchmarking is the practice of recognising and examining the best industrial and commercial practices in an industry or in the world and using this knowledge as the basis for improvement in all aspects of the business.

By monitoring best practice and comparing it with their own an organisation can identify areas where there is the potential for improvement. For example British Airways found that engineers from Japanese Airways took 40 minutes for maintenance checks on a Jumbo jet compared with BA's 3 hours. Productivity gains can be achieved in areas such as new product development, operational processes, management processes and distribution. **4 marks**

2. New technology could hinder the performance of the business because:

- the introduction of new technology might cause unrest amongst the employees affected because they have not been consulted; it breaks up established social groups or threatens job security
- people may be untrained and therefore unfamiliar with the new technology and hence work more slowly
- new technology is high risk and may not work or integrate properly with existing systems
- parallel running of new and old systems requires additional resources. **5 marks**

3. Factors affecting the location of a new factory include proximity to raw material, proximity to the market, availability of skilled labour, availability of cheap labour, availability of sites, climate and quality of life, transport links, political stability, government economic policies and incentives available. **3 marks**

4. Difficulties faced by a firm changing to a system of automated production include:

- raising finance to purchase new equipment
- loss of output – impact on profits and cashflow
- costs of training/retraining
- resistance to change
- demotivation due to breakup of social groups, insecurity and deskilling
- cost of redundancies
- possibility of teething problems with new system.
- reduced variety could cause problems for the marketing department. **3 marks**

 TIP

Consider the implications for each of the major functional departments.

5. Critical Path Analysis could be useful because:

■ it determines the earliest time that materials are needed in production and so suppliers can be notified of delivery times

■ it determines the latest time activities need to be started and so working capital can be minimised by avoiding unnecessary early starts

■ it identifies where slack (float time) exists within a schedule so that resources can be switched to complete a critical activity on time.

■ JIT relies on precise scheduling and control. CPA is a way of achieving that goal.   **6 marks**

Solutions to Paper 2, Part 3 (Case study)

Section A

David and Marcus have failed to reach agreement on the best course of action open to the company. They have requested you, a business consultant, to prepare a report for presentation to the Board of Directors. In particular the report should cover:

(a) an assessment of Babywear's current situation;

(b) an evaluation of each of the options under discussion.   **50 marks**

(a) an assessment of Babywear's current situation

 TIP

Did you realise you were required to consider non-financial information?

From the financial information you should be able to calculate and comment on the following ratios:

	1997	1996
Return on capital employed	13.45	16.25
Profit margin	21.69	25.74
Asset turnover	0.62	0.63
Liquidity ratio	1.3:1	1.5:1
Acid test ratio	0.6:1	1:1

The ratios show a decline in the return on capital employed, however, at present it is still reasonably healthy.

The decline in ROCE is overwhelmingly caused by the fall in the profit margin (itself caused by competition).

There has been a very unhealthy build-up of stock in the last year (product not competing on price?). The increase in stock has been broadly financed by an increase in short-term liabilities.

The liquidity ratio for 1996 is just acceptable (it should be in the range 1.5–2.0:1. For 1997 there is cause for concern.

The acid test ratio is an acceptable minimum for 1996 but dangerously low for 1997. More working capital is required if the firm is to pay its debts 'as and when they become due'.

Other comments arising from the case study and the statistical information could include:

■ Capacity utilisation has fallen from 90% to 70% in the last 10 years. What is also significant is that other producers now have a better utilisation ratio than Babywear (have they gone down the route of producing unbranded goods to offset the fall in demand for branded goods).

■ Overall size of the market has declined and the average amount spent by parents on baby clothes has also decreased.

■ All producers have raised prices by less than the rate of inflation over the last decade (result of increasing competition).

- The market is very price conscious (it is the single most important factor in the purchase decision according to the recent survey).
- The firm is becoming increasingly reliant on firms which have a smaller share of the market.
- Put together, all this information suggests that the firm is operating in an extremely competitive mature market. You could also argue that key elements of the marketing mix are wrong, for example the emphasis on high-quality branded goods, the promotion necessary to maintain the brand image and the high price required to support product and promotion. There is also evidence that the 'place' element of the mix is wrong.

TIP

The SWOT framework is very useful here.

(b) an evaluation of each of the options under discussion

The Pricerite proposal.

Points to make include:

- The company has the necessary spare capacity. Indeed, the problem of spare capacity may get worse!
- There is no effect on the Babywear brand name if the order is accepted.
- Whilst the profit margin is low the order does still contribute towards profits.
- The financing of the new machinery purchase could be problematic as a result of the problems indicated in the balance sheet.
- The contract requires a shift from batch to line production. The firm has no experience of this and indeed this might require staff redundancies or staff retraining. It will break up informal groups, reduce the level of morale and motivation in the factory affected and may even result in resistance to the change.
- The business has to change up to 25% of its productive capacity but is only guaranteed utilisation of 10% of that capacity under the contract.
- The proposal is not necessarily a long-term solution to the firm's problems but it does provide a breathing space while father and son consider the future (e.g. other segments of the clothing market).

The rationalisation proposal.

Points to make include:

- There is a significant amount of spare capacity.
- The Barnsley site could be sold easily and if expansion was required at a later date it could be accommodated at the other two sites.
- The company badly needs an injection of cash!
- A move like this could reduce costs significantly in the long run. However the savings in the short term would not be so great as costs (e.g. redundancy) would be incurred on closure.
- As an area of high unemployment there are significant social costs if the factory was closed.
- The proposal does little to address the problems that the firm is facing in the market place, namely: competition, a decline in the size of the market, the loss of major customers and the alienation of others, etc.

Knowledge, comprehension and application

LEVEL 1   Relevant material selected and presented appropriately. (Including 3 marks for report format.)   **(1–6 marks)**

LEVEL 2   Relevant material explained and presented appropriately.   **(7–10 marks)**

LEVEL 3   Relevant material explained fully, presented appropriately and applied to the case study.   **(11–16 marks)**

Analysis of evidence
LEVEL 1 Some analysis of information, but lacking insight or depth. **(1–4 marks)**

LEVEL 2 Substantial analysis using written and numerate techniques. **(5–9 marks)**

LEVEL 3 Substantial analysis using written and numerate techniques appropriately to identify causes or effects. **(10–12 marks)**

Synthesis
LEVEL 1 Report has a coherent structure. **(1–4 marks)**

LEVEL 2 Reports structure pulls points together, making it easy to follow the logic and recommendations. **(5–8 marks)**

Evaluation
LEVEL 1 Superficial attempt at drawing conclusions, relying on assertion rather than argument based on case. **(1–2 marks)**

LEVEL 2 Appropriate conclusions but without awareness of underlying themes. **(3–6 marks)**

LEVEL 3 Appropriate conclusions, showing awareness of underlying themes emerging from (or implicit within) the case. **(7–10 marks)**

LEVEL 4 Original conclusions drawn from the evidence, showing awareness of proximate and underlying themes and issues. **(11–14 marks)**

Section B

1. To what extent does forecasting enable an organisation to make better decisions? **25 marks**

LEVEL 1 Description of forecasting with little attempt to place in the context of the question. **(1–5 marks)**

LEVEL 2 Candidate attempts analysis but it lacks clarity, accuracy or depth. **(6–9 marks)**

LEVEL 3 Candidate analyses the question with accuracy and some depth. **(10–14 marks)**

LEVEL 4 Synthesis shown through logical sequencing and effective summarising of argument. **(15–18 marks)**

LEVEL 5 Evaluation/judgement based on own analysis. **(19–25 marks)**

Content
The reasons why forecasting enables an organisation to make better decisions include:

■ forecasting forces the organisation to collect information
■ it reduces the degree of subjectivity
■ the success rate of decisions made is likely to be improved
■ it reduces the likelihood that a powerful or charismatic employee can force through an unrealistic proposal/decision
■ enables decision to be justified.

The limitations of forecasting include:

■ decisions may be made on the basis of inaccurate information resulting from a poorly designed questionnaire or insufficient information
■ collection of data and analysis takes time and may result in opportunities being lost or slow response to threats
■ some decisions require a degree of creativity and/or risk and forecasting might inhibit the decision (e.g. Sony Walkman was rejected by market research).

2. (a)   **Explain why so many firms remain small.**   **10 marks**

      LEVEL 1   1 or more relevant points made superficially.   **(1–4 marks)**

      LEVEL 2   Fuller development of points made.   **(5–8 marks)**

      LEVEL 3   Evaluation of the relative importance of points.   **(9–10 marks)**

      Content
      Firms may remain small because:

- lack of finance
- limited product range
- lack of economies of scale
- owner wants to retain control – be his own boss, pass on to another member of the family
- demand is local or limited
- difficult to expand because providing a personal service
- difficult even to survive in todays competitive environment, let alone expand.

  (b)   **To what extent should the government step in to remedy this problem?**   **15 marks**

      LEVEL 1   Superficial attempt to answer the question based on relevant points.

                                                                   (1–4 marks)

      LEVEL 2   Some analysis of issues but underdeveloped.   **(5–8 marks)**

      LEVEL 3   Analysis of issues developed.   **(9–11 marks)**

      LEVEL 4   Judgement made on issues.   **(11–15 marks)**

      Content
      Themes could include:

- problems facing small firms provide a rationale for intervening
- level of help given by other governments to their small-firms sector again provides rationale
- free marketeers would argue not at all – must not distort markets
- patchy success of past attempts to help small firms suggests government should not intervene – waste of resources
- level playing field argument would suggest limited intervention where small firms at a disadvantage to large firms, e.g. areas such as raising capital, research and development and risk bearing.

3. (a)   **Discuss what documents an individual should provide to support an application for a bank loan to start up a business.**   **10 marks**

      LEVEL 1   Candidate identifes a number of documents relevant to an application for a bank loan.   **(1–4 marks)**

      LEVEL 2   Candidate makes some attempt at explaining why the documents are necessary.   **(5–7 marks)**

      LEVEL 3   Candidate offers a well developed explanation.   **(8–10 marks)**

      Content
      The principal documents would be:

- business plan
- cashflow forecast
- profit and loss account.

      The reasons for each of them would be:

- to determine how the business is going to be run and to evaluate the feasibilty of the proposal
- to check that sufficient cash is available to meet the needs of the business at all times
- to determine that the proposal is profitable.

(b) **Comment on the adequacy of these documents to assess an application for a loan.**

15 marks

LEVEL 1 Superficial attempt to answer the question based on 1 or more relevant points. **(1–4 marks)**

LEVEL 2 Fuller development of 2 or more points. **(5–8 marks)**

LEVEL 3 Clear ideas on the limitations of the documents and environmental/human uncertainties. **(9–12 marks)**

LEVEL 4 Judgement made on issues. **(13–15 marks)**

Content

Limitations of documents – underlying assumptions, e.g. value of stocks/debtors, extent of the market, level of sales that can be achieved.

Environmental uncertainty – economic (level of competition, implications of a slowdown in economic activity/rise in inflation/changes in exchange rate), social (changes in attitudes, demographic changes), political (new legislation, change in government), technology (implications for product and processes).

Human factors – must consider the applicant's personality, track record and commitment.

4. (a) **Distinguish between job and batch production systems.** **5 marks**

LEVEL 1 Candidate has identified 1 or more relevant points. **(1–3 marks)**

LEVEL 2 Candidate has explained 1 or more relevant factors. **(4–5 marks)**

The differences include:

	job	batch
size of order	small	larger
volume of output	low	greater
product range	large	lower
process flexibility	very high	lower
machinery	general purpose	more specialist
labour skill	high	lower

(b) **How might a bread manufacturer gain from changing production processes from batch to flow?** **10 marks**

LEVEL 1 Candidate identifes 1 or more of gains but with little explanation or development. **(1–4 marks)**

LEVEL 2 Candidate makes some attempt at explaining how the gains have arisen. **(5–7 marks)**

LEVEL 3 Candidate offers a well-developed explanation. **(8–10 marks)**

Gains could include:

■ unit cost reductions through production economies of scale (give examples)
■ other economies of scale in marketing, finance and personnel
■ product standardisation
■ mechanisation of process
■ hygiene and quality issues.

(c) **What problems do you think might arise as a result of such a change?** **10 marks**

LEVEL 1 Candidate identifes 1 or more problems with little explanation or development. **(1–3 marks)**

LEVEL 2 Candidate makes some attempt at explaining why the points identified are problems. **(4–7 marks)**

LEVEL 3 Candidate offers a well developed explanation of the points identified. **(8–10 marks)**

Problems include:

- human factors including reaction to change, need to retrain, nature of jobs provided (link to motivation), turnover and absenteeism
- raising of necessary finance for new machinery and equipment
- loss of production flexibility
- high cost of breakdown
- need for stable level of demand throughout year and a long product life cycle.

5. **Strikes are a thing of the past!**
   (a) **Discuss this statement.** **10 marks**

   LEVEL 1 Vague attempt to answer the question based on superficial knowledge of facts. **(1–4 marks)**

   LEVEL 2 Fuller discussion of 1 or more points. **(5–8 marks)**

   LEVEL 3 Evaluation of statement. **(9–10 marks)**

   Content
   The grounds for this statement are the published statistics which show the incidence of strikes is far less than in the 50s, 60s and 70s. However, the statement is very sweeping. Workers do still go on strike and the disputes are sometimes long and very bitter. It is also very difficult to predict the future and it is possible to envisage circumstances in which the incidence of strikes could rise (changes in legislation/attitudes of workers/economic circumstances).

   (b) **To what extent does this indicate an improvement in British industrial relations?** **15 marks**

   LEVEL 1 Superficial attempt to answer the question based on relevant points. **(1–4 marks)**

   LEVEL 2 Some analysis of issues but underdeveloped. One-sided argument will gain a maximum of 8 marks. **(5–8 marks)**

   LEVEL 3 Developed arguments considering both sides of the argument. **(9–12 marks)**

   LEVEL 4 Evaluation of statement. **(11–15 marks)**

   Content
   Strikes are only one form of industrial action and it would be necessary to consider trends in these other forms of action as well before drawing any conclusions.

   One point of view would be to accept the statement and draw attention to the changes of the last 15–20 years. Legislation has been introduced to curb the power of trade unions. Traditional industries with high trade union membership have declined and newer industries with fewer workers and no history of unionisation have grown. Trade union membership has slumped dramatically. In many firms there has also been a movement toward better labour relations practices, often through the introduction of Japanese management techniques such as lean production. Involvement in decision-making, greater control of work and greater responsibility are powerful motivators for many people.

   An alternative viewpoint would be to argue that fewer strikes do not indicate the improvement suggested. Workers don't go on strike now because they are scared they will lose their jobs. There is less protection for strikers now and for trade unions. If the law was different and it was also easier to get another job workers might be more inclined to strike. Indeed, due to the lack of power workers now have, employers have been able to introduce new work practices requiring the employee to work far harder than before.

6. **Increasing numbers of people are working from home rather than the office.**
   (a) **Explain why this has happened.**   **10 marks**

   > **LEVEL 1**   Has identified 1 or more relevant points superficially.   **(1–5 marks)**

   > **LEVEL 2**   Has explained 1 or more relevant points.   **(6–10 marks)**

   Content
   - identification of technology that enables working from home to occur, e.g. computer workstations, fax machines, the Internet, phones, teleconferencing, etc.
   - reducing cost and greater power of information technology
   - cost of office space versus costs of working from home
   - changing social attitudes to commuting and office work
   - enables parent to combine child rearing and working.

   (b) **Assess whether this trend is likely to continue.**   **15 marks**

   > **LEVEL 1**   Has identified 1 or more relevant points on one side of the argument.   **(1–3 marks)**

   > **LEVEL 2**   Has identified 1 or more relevant points on each side of the argument but the treatment is superficial.   **(4–6 marks)**

   > **LEVEL 3**   Developed points considering both sides of the argument.   **(7–9 marks)**

   > **LEVEL 4**   Evaluates points and makes a balanced argument for future.   **(10–15 marks)**

   Content
   Trend may continue because:
   - knowledge-based industries (which are likely to be growth sectors) lend themselves to homeworking
   - IT costs likely to continue decreasing
   - output will become less paper-based
   - social trends re. commuting and combining parenting and career likely to continue.

   Trend may not continue because:
   - difficulties in controlling the homeworker
   - people go to work for social reasons
   - a long way to go before the paperless office.